Fools and Folly

Fools and Folly

Edited by
Clifford Davidson

Early Drama, Art, and Music
Monograph Series, 22

MEDIEVAL INSTITUTE PUBLICATIONS

WESTERN MICHIGAN UNIVERSITY

Kalamazoo, Michigan
1996

Cover Design by Linda Judy

ISBN 1-879288-69-9 (Casebound)
ISBN 1-879288-70-2 (Paperbound)

Contents

Illustrations

Introduction

Clifford Davidson

In Charles Williams' thriller *The Greater Trumps,* the fortune-telling card known as the Fool in the Tarot deck is identified as "sovereign or . . . nothing, and if it is nothing then man was born dead."[1] In Williams' image theology the Fool represents either what is most dominant or what is most insignificant in the cosmos—and in the end dominance is affirmed. This figure among the Tarot cards thus is a representative of and a participant in the cosmic dance which is at the center of all things. The Fool is not in this modern author's view to be truly equated with folly, which is the foolishness of persons living in this world and performing those futile deeds described long ago in Sebastian Brant's *Narrenschiff* and Alexander Barclay's English adaptation, *The Ship of Fools,* initially published in 1509 by Pynson. Nor is Williams' Fool a candidate to be entered as one of the fraternity described by John Lydgate in "A Tale of Thre skore ffoolys and thre wich are lyk neuer ffor to the,"[2] for instead he is to be regarded as a symbol of uniqueness —i.e., not as one who would appear among the throng of charlatans and ne'er-do-wells of Lydgate's poem.

For Lydgate, the chief of fools is one "that nouther loveth God nor dredith,/ Nor to his chirche hath noon advertence,/ Nor to his seyntys doth no reuerence . . ." (ll. 11–13). Further, he refuses aid to the poor and fails to respect his father and mother. This, then, is also the fool who appears in illuminations appearing at the head of Psalm 52 (*AV*: 53) in English psalters where the verse "The fool said in his heart: There is no God" is followed by the statement "They are corrupted, and become abominable in iniquities: there is none that doth good." These illuminations normally show the fool as the denier of God before a king, or they provide variants on this theme, as in the case of the *Bromholm Psalter* (Oxford, Bodleian Library, MS. Ashmole 1523, fol. 66) where the fool is arguing with a righteous man.[3] Most interesting of all perhaps is a late manuscript, the *Psalter of Henry VIII*, where King Henry is depicted as the reigning monarch who, in imitation of King David, is playing his harp, while his fool Will Sommers is turning away from him (Royal MS. 2.A.XVI, fol. 63^{v}).[4] In none of these cases does the fool represent anything but folly, though such folly may indeed be found entertaining to persons at the courts of kings—i.e., persons who, as in the case of Henry VIII, flatter themselves that they are sophisticated—and elsewhere. The idea of the fool was also part of the popular imagination.

The behavior that is satirized in Lydgate's poem involves both the frivolous, described as "More than a fooll, braynles, maad, and wood" (l. 18), and the vicious. The latter include the deceitful, unstable, covetous, quarrelsome, and so forth. Additionally, there are the hypocritical ones, who, for example, would "With ful wombe [i.e., stomach] . . . preche of abstynence" (l. 161). Lydgate's fools are under the patronage of Bishop Nullatensis—a reminder that the number for a fool is nought in medieval tradition. So, therefore, in the morality play of *Mankind* the triumvirate Nought, Nowadays, and Newguise all act foolishly enough, though it is Nought who apparently was actually costumed like a fool.[5] Nought loves "well to be mery" and has "pleyde so longe the foll" that he has even made himself tired of his act (ll. 273–75).

Charles Williams' Fool, on the other hand, can only be understood in terms of the paradox presented by St. Paul, who proclaimed that "We are fools for Christ's sake . . ." (*1 Corinthians* 4.10). The idea that those who are "of the world" will see the faithful one as a fool is not, of course, only to be found in Williams' Neoplatonizing philosophy, for it was a theological notion current in the late Middle Ages as well. For example, in the York plays,[6] Christ himself is affirmed to be a "fole kyng" (XXXIV.28) and is otherwise many times called a fool by his torturers. The "fool king" would have been a figure in a Christmas game, as Sandra Billington has indicated: in Play XXXI, "Herod presumes Christ to be the local Fool-entertainer or magician and looks forward to seeing water turned into wine and the dead brought to life."[7] Those who expect such foolery are naturally confounded as Christ remains silent, but, as Billington notes, his placement in the scene along with an actual king, albeit the tyrant Herod, is in fact reminiscent of the psalter illustrations with the king and the fool appearing together. In the end the silent Christ is taken to be a natural rather than an artificial fool.[8] The ironic hail lyrics spoken by the torturers in the Tilemakers' play (XXXIII.408–16) not only stand in direct contrast to the hail lyrics of the shepherds at the scene of the Nativity in the Towneley *Secunda Pastorum*[9] but also are indicative of the role of the fool king as perceived by Christ's torturers.[10] These lyrics in the York play have come after the scene of the mock crowning. The crowning is introduced by the Second Soldier, who cries out, "O fule, how faris þou now?" (*York* XXXIII.387). The Third Soldier responds: "Nowe because he oure kyng gon hym call/ We will kyndely hym croun with a brere," while the Fourth Soldier adds, "Ʒa, but first þis purpure and palle/ And þis worthy wede sall he were,/ For scorne" (ll. 388–92).

Ultimately the torturers' willingness to see Christ as a fool will demonstrate their inability to come to a recognition of either his humanity or his divinity. Through such misperception Christ can become for them a scapegoat figure that in their view is worthy only of being beaten and scourged and thereafter crucified. The audience, however, is invited to empathize deeply with the one who is thus tortured and executed. While one of Herod's courtiers believes that Christ will be found to be "fonne in his folie" (*York* XXXI.360), the real madness and folly lies among his accusers and torturers. At the Last Day the Savior will return "To make endyng of mannes folie" (*York* XLVII.56), but those who have with seeming foolishness according to his Word followed Christ will be among the men and women spared from the everlasting bonfire.

The interpretation of the Christian fool had been affirmed by St. Bernard of Clairvaux, who saw this fool in terms of the professional entertainer of his time:

> We are like jesters and tumblers, who, with heads down and feet up, exhibit extraordinary behaviour by standing or walking on their hands, and thus draw all eyes to themselves. But ours is not the play of children or of the theatre, which excites lust and represents sordid acts in the effeminate and shameful contortions of actors. No, ours is a joyous game, decent, grave, and admirable, delighting the gaze of the heavenly onlookers. This chaste and religious game he plays who says: "We are made a spectacle to angels and to men" (1 Cor. 4:9). And let us too play this game now, so that we may be made game of, humbled, until he comes who casts down the mighty and exalts the humble, who will gladden us, glorify us, and exalt us forever.[11]

For Bernard, the fool identity as applied to the follower of Christ is not a sign of a world upside down as much as it is a sign of his humility.[12] Yet significantly this fool is an exhibitionist—a model of self-display that in fact resides not actually in the person's attempt to "show off" but in his acceptance of a role in the stage play of life in which he makes visible a life-pattern at distinct variance with the conventional.

A connection may be made here with the fool figure as he appears in the plays of the greatest dramatist of the English language. Shakespeare's fools—e.g., the Fool in *King Lear*—will serve to amuse and yet teach, often however through irony, as when Lear's companion advises, "Let go thy hold when a great wheel runs down a hill, lest it break thy neck with following; but the great one that goes upward, let him draw thee after" (II.iii.71–75).[13] These words represent a prudential ethic that points back in an inverted way to the "foolishness" of Cordelia. The youngest sister's imprudent goodness is scorned by her worldly sisters, who are focused on power and, at least at times, motivated by lust. The Fool in this instance bears all the complexity of his derivation from the paradoxical idea of the fool inherited from the Middle Ages. In the world upside down of this play,[14] the value of the Fool is that he articulates the way of inversion that proves the rightness of Cordelia's choice.

But Shakespeare is writing not only in the wake of the increased popularity of the fool in English courts—from Will Sommers and Cardinal Wolsey's Patch to Richard Tarlton and King James' Archie Armstrong—but also after the publication in English translation of that long ironic panegyric to foolishness under the title *The Praise of Folly*.[15] This work by Desiderius Erasmus, who dedicated his original Latin text to Sir Thomas More under the ironic title *Encomium Moriae*, presented a sophisticated mock defense of foolish behavior as preferable to rational acts. Lear's Fool in his speech advising grasping hold of the wheel that goes up the hill rather than down—that is, hanging onto the one whose fortunes are rising rather than falling—is of a piece with Erasmus' personification of Folly.

In the Middle Ages and subsequently, the fool is a paradoxical figure of the greatest complexity who deserves to be examined from different perspectives. Several perspectives are offered in the articles collected in the present volume. In no case prior to the modern period is Folly presented with the glowingly positive qualities afforded the Tarot Fool in Charles Williams' novel, but there is a recognition at least from time to time that the way of the cross possesses an absurdity and a devotion to humility that set it off from the pride of the great men of this world or from the ways of the secular sphere.

Thus in the essays which follow in the present volume Sandra Billington (University of Glasgow) calls attention to the symbolism of the humble ass and to the inversion which, at Lyon especially in the *cheval fol*, asserts the folly of the pretensions of the proud. Martin Walsh (University of Michigan) writes about a king, Robert of Sicily, that in his pride is put down and made to take on the role of a fool, who thus suffers all the derision of the ridiculed fool of medieval courts.[16] This article provides valuable documentation concerning the attitudes toward "natural" fools —i.e., fools who, in distinction from the self-fashioned or "artificial" fools, were born that way. Ironically, such natural fools were likely to have been seen as covered by the doctrine of "invincible ignorance" described by St. Thomas Aquinas, in which case they were expected to be admitted to bliss after death since on account of mental deficiency they could not be expected to understand the crucial points of Christian doctrine.[17]

Alexander Barclay's *Ship of Fools* is discussed by Robert C. Evans (Auburn University at Montgomery), who indicates the importance of this work for understanding the "fault lines" present in the social fabric of the times and who argues for study in more depth of this work, which was extremely influential throughout the early modern period. Peter Happé (University of Southampton), in turn, gives attention to the depiction of the fool in the early Tudor theater, especially concentrating on John Heywood and Sir David Lindsay, while W. N. M. Hüsken (Nijmegen) takes up the role of the fool as a social critic in the Dutch Rhetoricians' drama. Ultimately the Dutch fools, he concludes, were "not foolish at all" since they taught by example "how to avoid being carried away in ships of fools" of the types specified by Sebastian Brant in his *Narrenschiff*. Robert W. Leslie (North Glasgow College) rounds out the volume with an article on fools in the Renaissance in which he focuses on the development of the tradition of the Sienese fool in Italy and his reappearance in the drama of Renaissance England.

NOTES

[1] Charles Williams, *The Greater Trumps* (1950; rpt. New York: Farrar, Straus, and Cudahy, 1962), p. 227.

[2] John Lydgate, *The Minor Poems*, Pt. II, ed. Henry Noble MacCracken, EETS, o.s. 192 (1934; rpt. London: Oxford Univ. Press, 1961), pp. 449–55.

For another example in which fools are associated with vices, see Hans Sachs' carnival play *Das Narren-Schneyden* (*Fool Surgery*), in which a mountebank doctor removes seven fools from the belly of a gullible peasant. These fools are the Seven Deadly Sins. For discussion of this play, see Ralf Erik Remshardt, "The Birth of Reason from the Spirit of Carnival: Hans Sachs and *Das Narren-Schneyden*," *Comparative Drama*, 23 (1989), 70–94.

[3] See Clifford Davidson, *Illustrations of the Stage and Acting in England to 1580*, Early Drama, Art, and Music, Monograph Ser., 16 (Kalamazoo: Medieval Institute Publications, 1991), fig. 76; see also ibid., pp. 67–79, for further commentary on the fool in psalter illustrations.

[4] Ibid., fig. 89.

[5] Clifford Davidson, *Visualizing the Moral Life: Medieval Iconography and the Macro Moralities* (New York: AMS Press, 1989), pp. 26–27; for another view, see Sandra Billington, "'Suffer Fools Gladly': The Fool in Medieval England and the Play *Mankind*," in *The Fool and the Trickster*, ed. Paul V. A. Williams (Cambridge: D. S. Brewer, 1979), pp. 42–44.

[6] *The York Plays*, ed. Richard Beadle (London: Edward Arnold, 1982); quotations from the York plays and other medieval plays are identified in my text by play and line numbers.

[7] Sandra Billington, *A Social History of the Fool* (Brighton: Harvester Press, 1984), pp. 18–19. In the York play, Herod will (in response to Christ's refusal to play the game) himself play the fool (see ibid., p. 19). In this case we can identify Herod's role playing as that of an "artificial" fool.

[8] Ibid., p. 19.

[9] *The Towneley Plays*, ed. Martin Stevens and A. C. Cawley, EETS, s.s. 13–14 (Oxford: Oxford Univ. Press, 1994), I, 126–57.

[10] See Billington, *A Social History of the Fool*, pp. 19–20.

[11] Bernard of Clairvaux, *Letters*, trans. B. Scott James (Chicago: Henry H. Regnery, 1953), p. 130, as quoted by John Saward, *Perfect Fools: Folly for Christ's Sake in Catholic and Orthodox Spirituality* (Oxford: Oxford Univ. Press, 1980), p. 58.

[12] Saward, *Perfect Fools*, pp. 59–60. See also Jacopone da Todi, who affirmed that the "highest wisdom is to be thought mad for the love of Christ" (quoted in translation in ibid., p. 89).

[13] Quotations from Shakespeare are from *The Riverside Shakespeare*, gen. ed. G. Blakemore Evans (Boston: Houghton Mifflin, 1974).

[14] See my article "The Iconography of Wisdom and Folly in *King Lear*," in *Shakespeare and the Emblem*, ed. Tibor Fabiny, Papers in English and American Studies, 3 (Szeged, Hungary: Dept. of English, Attila József Univ., 1984), pp.

189–214.

[15] See Desiderius Erasmus, *The Praise of Folly*, trans. John Wilson [1688] (Ann Arbor: Univ. of Michigan Press, 1958). For Erasmus, the principal characteristic of Folly is self-love. This characteristic is given visual expression in Holbein's illustration of Folly as a fool examining its own image in its bauble; see F. Saxl, "Holbein's Illustration to the *Praise of Folly* by Erasmus," *Burlington Magazine*, 83 (1943), 276. On the other hand, Holbein's illustration for the scene of the woman kneeling and placing a candle before the Virgin—a candle not needed in the daylight—counteracts the irony of Erasmus' text; the woman's sincerity in the artist's depiction seems to identify her as one of the foolish ones who paradoxically are in fact the most wise. See ibid., p. 276, Pl. I.F.

[16] For an example in which a court fool was ridiculed in a strange way, see *The Staging of Religious Drama in Europe in the Later Middle Ages*, ed. Peter Meredith and John E. Tailby, Early Drama, Art, and Music, Monograph Ser., 4 (Kalamazoo: Medieval Institute Publications, 1983), pp. 94–95. In 1414 Borra, the jester of King Ferdinand of Aragon, was deliberately frightened by a special effect produced as part of the coronation banquet when he was confronted with a figure of Death that was being lowered from above, whereupon the jester was caught by a rope thrown down around him by Death and pulled up as if to meet his end. The fool was so terrified that he urinated, and the urine ran onto the heads of those who were sitting below. According to the report, the "King watched all this and was greatly amused, as were all the others" (p. 95).

[17] A former colleague, James Thayer, reported to me that in certain areas in West Africa persons who are mentally deficient are regarded as close to God; hence they are encouraged to beg, and are given small amounts of money when they come to one's door.

The *Cheval fol* of Lyon and Other Asses

Sandra Billington

In the Middle Ages many animals came to symbolize qualities or faults in human beings, and many domesticated animals such as the dog, horse, and little ass or donkey could be invested with either a virtue or a vice, depending on the context—for example, the dog as an example of either treachery or fidelity.[1] Because of the horse's courage, spirit, and loyalty to the master who had tamed it, it too was often considered exemplary to the point of anthropomorphosis, as in the well-known twelfth-century *Bestiary* translated by T. H. White (Cambridge University Library MS. II.4.26), where it is said, uniquely, to "weep for man and feel the emotion of sorrow. And hence in Centaurs the nature of men and horses can be mixed." Horses "exult in battlefields; . . . they are excited to the fight by the sound of a trumpet. Inflamed by the war-yell, they are spurred to charge. They are miserable when conquered and delighted when they have won."[2]

A rather different outcome of such perceived volatility was another association between the horse and wilful folly. The ungoverned animal was said to be driven by selfish desires, oblivious to the destruction it caused. In the twelfth-century *Virtues and Vices*, a dialogue between Reason and the Soul, Reason gives the following warning against the whole gamut of sins: "When thoughts of avidity, or of luxury, or of covetousness, or of wrath, and of envy and indignation, or of vain boasting, or of haughtiness and pride come to thee, know thou forsooth that it is the devil. . . . 'Be not like the horse or the mule, which have no understanding'."[3] This quotation from Psalm 31.9

(*AV*: 32.9) equates these two beasts with all the vices because of their response to will rather than intellect, and in England such equine folly was often given the name of Charlemagne's Bayard. For example, in the *Tale of Beryn* the blind man accuses Beryn of stealing his eyes and, using the words of a proverb, regrets earlier help offered to him: "a man to seruesabill/ Ledith offt[e] beyard from his owne stabill"[4]—i.e., a man too helpful to another often nurtures a destructive horse. In Gower's *Confessio Amantis* the effects of love are compared with the recklessness of a blind horse: "farewell God and Law;/ He cannot recognize their force;/ But like Bayard, the blinded horse,/ He answers no man's hand at all/ Till plump into the ditch they fall."[5] Such a creature only learns by harsh experience, and Chaucer's Troilus is the classic example. Troilus too is blind in the recklessness of his passion for Cressyde; turning himself into a fool who will not keep to the proper road:

> O blynde world, O blynde entencioun!
> How often falleth al the effect contraire
> Of surquidrie and foul presumpcioun;
>
> . . .
>
> This Troilus is clomben on the staire
> And litel weneth that he moot descenden;
> But alday faileth thing that fooles wenden.
>
> As proude Bayard gynneth for to skippe
> Out of the weye, so pryketh hym his corn,
> Til he a lasshe have of the longe whippe. . . .
> (*Troilus and Cressyde* I.211–13, 215–20)[6]

Troilus here is totally unromantic—going his own way, climbing a stair without realizing that he must descend, for what fools undertake always fails. The caveat is set at the opening of the poem, clarifying for the reader that, no matter how sympathetic he might appear, Troilus is an example of folly to be avoided.

French dictionaries do not reveal a similar development for the name 'Bayard'; in the sources cited the animal retains his original identity.[7] But the festive custom of the *cheval fol,* performed at Lyon from the fifteenth century to the seventeenth century, featured an animal suffering from the same malaise. The context was a political one—that is, revolts against the change in the city's power-base away from the Cathedral Chapter, which was supported by the plebeians, to the bourgeoisie supported by the King of France. An immediate result was an increase in taxation and near famine for the lower classes as their power decreased.

The Lyon historian Guillaume Paradin recorded three rebellions,[8] the last at Pentecost in 1436. All artisans except those from the Quarter of Bourgchanin looted their way through the city and would have destroyed a sacred, even mythological symbol where folklore and Church lore combined—the Abbey at Ainey at the confluence of the two rivers. The people of Bourgchanin defended the Abbey and in reward were given the festival of the *Cheval fol* at Pentecost explicitly to mock the ambitious folly of the rebels, *"qui faisant les folz et eschappez, avoient voulu trencher des roys."*[9] The word 'king' is interesting since it is not strictly relevant to the political situation; it mythologizes the issue with an archetypal symbol of power, as demonstrated in the festival.

A man inside a hobby horse but otherwise dressed as a king, with crown, peruke, cape, and upright sword,[10] led a burlesque procession through the city. This centaur, accompanied by a cacophonous orchestra and cavorting through the streets, performed outrageous and unpredictable pranks with the crowd. The festival ended at Ainay where a wooden or straw model of the man-horse was burned and dropped into the river[11] (fig. 1). The custom could look like a fertility rite (such as that at Padstow), and it has been claimed as one;[12] but behind this demonstration of animal energy was mockery of the folly of the temporary fool-king who fell to oblivion after his one day of misrule. Sixteenth-century verses make this clear:

Quant à ce cheval fol, qui sautille, qui danse,
Qui, du son des hautbois, cabriole en cadence,
C'est en derision de ces fols mutinés,
Qui, comme chevaux fols, couraient parmi la ville,
Voulant à qui mieux paraitre plus habil,
A s'enrichir des biens qu'ils avaient butinés.[13]

(What is this cheval fol, who leaps, who dances,
Who to the sound of the hautbois capers in rhythm;
It's mockery of these rebellious fools
Who, like crazy horses, run through the town
Wanting to enrich themselves with goods plundered from
the more able.)

Like Bayard—and like the horse in Alciati's emblem (fig. 2),[14] the *cheval fol* is said to follow its self-centered and destructive instincts. Such wayward creatures and the men they represent need to be more firmly bridled.

The horse is one of the most able and gifted of animals therefore potentially all the more dangerous. By contrast, the ass is the least gifted, but it too could be given either a positive or a negative character, though in this case both were aspects of harmless fool-behavior. The negative is the most common; there are no secular accolades at all for the ass in, for example, Erasmus' *Adages* or Alciati's *Emblematum Liber*. At best the animal is used as an example of the toughness that stupidity sometimes shows in enduring against the odds. Occasionally it was contrasted with the horse, as in the proverbs "from horses to asses," when a man went from an honorable to a disreputable profession, and "the plodding donkeys have produced a horse," to mean, among other things, a proud, bold man of low-born parents.[15] In secular literature, the donkey without exception seems to have been credited only with the absurd and harmless attributes of a poor mentality. The *Bestiary* explains:

People captured the Donkey by the following stratagem. Being forsooth a tardy beast and having no sense at all, it surrendered as soon as men surrounded it! . . . The little Ass, though smaller than the Wild Ass, is more useful, because it puts up with work and does not take exception to almost unlimited neglect.[16]

This plasticity allowed men to domesticate them earlier than the highly sensitive horse, and contempt is summed up in the *Middle English Dictionary* definition of "dull and uncomprehending."

However, several religious works make clear that Jesus chose such a humble animal deliberately[17] and "mekely rod on a sympyll asse-backe"[18] for his entry into Jerusalem. Some—e.g., the writer of the thirteenth-century *Ormulum*—claim that Christ's crib was the stall of an ass, although the *New Testament* only says a manger.[19] St. Augustine further uses *Isaiah* 1.3 as a prophecy that Christ's first bed would be the ass's crib.[20] In the *Cursor Mundi* Christ is given the words "þe meke asse þat ȝe þere fynde:/ Soone þat ȝe hir vndo./ Out of hir bonde. . . ,"[21] which hint at ultimate rewards in heaven. In the *Vices and Virtues* the ass is implicitly used as a moral contrast with the horse and mule (mentioned above). The Soul instructs: "But one ought to do with [the body] as with the ass . . . that it may tell this truth: 'I am made as a beast toiling before Thee, that I may rest with Thee',"[22] which also promises heavenly rewards for the meek. In many of these moral works the donkey's lack of self-awareness becomes a parallel for Pauline folly—the fool for Christ's sake who is not wise after his own flesh—though in the *Ormulum* there is a more secular metaphor; its stupidity is an analogy for mankind's, thus emphasizing Christ's generosity in adopting such an ignorant shape: "The Lord Jesus Christ was laid in an ass's crib, signifying to us that he became man on earth; man who was foolish, slow, ignorant, like an ass."[23]

In the *Legenda Aurea* elaborate comparison is made between the humility of this nativity and Adam's pride that reached as high as did Satan's,[24] and the evidence below suggests that churchmen and their playwrights also used the two animals to symbolize a central theological opposition between Pauline and satanic folly. Some homilies make an explicit contrast between the humility of the ass and the pride of the horse, particularly in sermons on Christ's entry into Jerusalem—for example, in Mirk's *Festial*[25] and in the Old English Homily for Palm Sunday which explains more elaborately:

> [Our Lord] might ride, if he desired, on rich steeds, and palfreys, mules, and Arabs, but he would not, nor even upon the big ass, but upon the little foal that was still suckling—nor had ever borne any burden, nor had ever been defiled by any other ass. In so great humility did God Almighty place himself for us, and moreover set us example, that when we have wealth in abundance in this life be ye not therefore proud, nor wild (elated), nor stark (haughty), nor wayward, nor highminded.[26]

Three of the last adjectives above could well apply to the horse of the opening of the quotation. The warning against the folly of imperiling the soul for worldly desires is expressed in terms associated with the wilful animal: the failings of man and beast appear to be combined, centaur-like, with the horse an embodiment of the rider's error. Similarly, Christ's choice, the ass's foal, symbolizes his own humility and innocence.

English mystery cycles and French Passion plays often bring the ass on stage to be ridden by characters epitomizing Christian humility. In the Chester cycle it is implied that Mary and Joseph travel with it to Bethlehem for the census since Mary asks to be lifted down on arrival, and stage directions at the birth read: "Tunc statuet Mariam inter bovem et asinam" (Play VI.468 *s.d.*).[27] Before the Flight into Egypt, Joseph says to her, "upon my asse shall thou sytt" (X.274), and before the Entry into Jerusalem, as one would expect, "Jesus sedens super asellam" (XIV.208 *s.d.*). The illustrations showing each day of the Valenciennes play (performed in 1547) depict the ass in these three scenes, and Gréban also has Mary travel to Bethlehem on the animal which remains with them until the Flight. Today the ass evokes humility, but originally the associations could have been stronger; it could have symbolized the apparent absurdity of God born (and dying) in the most worthless context, and, as the *Ormulum* attempts to explain, God's lack of concern for worldly values became the Christian folly defined by Paul.

Another place where we know an ass was used was in Beauvais Cathedral in the twelfth century at the Epiphany ceremony of Mary's flight into Egypt, and this is the context most associated with it: the inverted religious environment of the *asinaria festa*, a version of the Feast of Fools. The festival sometimes began on Holy Innocents' day and, at Beauvais, could extend to 14 January so as to include Mary's flight, although the true New Year Kalends were on 1 January. Reports on the mid-winter Church festival reveal a constant tussle between the Christianization of the pagan and the secularization of the Christian. As Augustine's Christmas Sermons show, both solstices were turned into appropriate Christian alternatives,[28] and, although he makes no comment, the inversions of the Saturnalia are also reflected in the celebration of a vulnerable infant who was to overcome kings. It would be strange if the Church Fathers had not been conscious of such a parallel at the same time as they showed their severity towards the original custom of the January Kalends: "The first of January is coming. You are all Christians. . . . Let nothing happen that is odious to God—iniquitous games, shameless amusements. . . . Your Bishop is forewarning you. I warn you, I state publicly, I make this an official declaration. Hear your Bishop commanding you! . . . let no-one do it!"[29]

The ass's incorporation into the Church festival could have expressed lower clergy defiance of such injunctions since seasonal inversion demanded the exaltation of the most foolish animal, or it could have been a way of taming the clerics' alternative antics with an animal symbolic of Christ's own humility. Twelfth- and thirteenth-century reforms of the *festa fatuorum* suggest that mayhem had been a part. The verse *Deposuit potentes de sede et exaltavit humiles* ("he hath put down the mighty from their seats, and hath exalted the humble and meek") had been "hailed with inordinate repetition by the delighted throng of inferior clergy," who were limited to five repetitions only and were ordered to remain properly in their stalls for the whole of the Feast[30]—a hint that previously they had taken over the church in a physical demonstration of their liberation. At about the same time, Pope Innocent III issued a decree against masks and other theatrical additions to the Festival of Fools, including mad, derisive, and obscene bacchantic gestures; further, as Margot Fassler shows, it was this festival, held on 1 January, which gave the authorities "the greatest cause for worry."[31]

The wildest known *asinaria festa* was at Beauvais also in the twelfth century, with the Flight into Egypt its focus: the ass was censed with black pudding and sausages (according to Erasmus the ordinary man's symbol of cornucopia[32]). The sung Mass which followed included brays as responses to the Introit, *Kyrie*, *Gloria*, and *Credo*. Chambers notes a rubric specifying that the "celebrant, instead of saying *Ite, missa est*, shall bray three times and . . . the people shall respond in similar fashion."[33] The extant *asinaria* text from Sens, though, appears to have been part of Pierre de Corbeil's reformed practices, without the sausages and the braying but allowing the ass its glorification as *Asinorum Dominus, Sire, pulcher, fortissimus,* and *belle bouche*. One of the offices attributed to de Corbeil is as follows: "Lux hodie, lux laetitiae, me iudice tristis quisquis erit, removendum solemnibus istis, sint hodie procul invidiae, procul omnia maesta, laeta volunt, quicumque colunt asinaria festa" ("Light of today, light of gladness. I order that whoever is sad shall be removed from these celebrations. Let ill-will be far distant today and sorrow. Whoever cares for the Feast of Asses wishes for joy").[34] As Chambers has noted, this has a simple dignity.

Fifteenth-century evidence for the *festa fatuorum* shows that the human Dominus could also be subjected to the reverse humilation of being put down—at Sens water was poured over the *Precentor stultorum* on the evening of his election[35]—and it could be that inclusion of the ass had resulted in a less aggressive form of folly. Its direct association with Christ, and additionally the date of its appearance, could have helped to temper the proceedings, in which case it would have been the appearance of the creature itself in the church and the process of honoring it that created a more controlled absurdity. It may be observed that, although docile, asses often run berserk if startled.

These customs celebrated the lowly at the lowest point of the year and turned them into temporary lords, while the *Cheval fol* appeared at an appropriate summer season, when satire was often directed at lordly and self-centered aspirations. Chaucer too appears to include a summertime of youthful kingship for Troilus. Repeatedly he is referred to as proud—"as proud as a pekok" (I.210), "proude knight" (I.225)—and, as noted, Chaucer comments: "How often falleth al the effect contraire/ Of surquidrie and foul presumpcioun!" (I.212–13). As stated in the passage previously quoted, "Troilus is clomben on the staire/ And litel weneth that he moot descenden." The rise only to fall equates the stair with Fortune's wheel: in *The Times Whistle* the stair's summit is referred to as the pinnacle of man's achievement.[36] For Troilus, Cressyde is to be the temporary summit of his life, arrived at through Fortune's intervention: "thus Fortune a tyme ledde in joie/ Criseyde and ek this kynges sone of Troie" (III.1714–15). Fortune, the temporary summit, and his regal status combine to suggest that Troilus is a fool-king in the midsummer of his life;[37] vigor and pride raise him in love before they ruin him. The folly of wayward aspirations and temporary kingship in the *cheval fol* and in Troilus appear in association with a real or metaphorical summertime.[38] Mirk's homily for Palm Sunday, cited above and quoted in my note 25, also mentions a height of worldly exaltation in association with the pride of riding on horseback, and some of the attack is against literally raising the height of the rider. Christ's entry into Jerusalem was a paradoxical event which could have been misunderstood as a moment of pride since he was a man at an age of physical strength —i.e., in the summertime of his youth—received as King in worldly terms and given a triumphant progress through the city of Jerusalem. Riding an ass helped to contradict the power symbolism, and could explain why homilies made such pointed distinctions between riding either animal.

The same distinctions appear in medieval dramas, which not only include the ass where relevant but also introduce the horse's negative associations as an appropriate reflection on its rider. The prime example is found in *The Conversion of St. Paul* in the Digby manuscript.[39] This play opens with Saul dressed as an "*aunterous knyght*"[40] arrogantly boasting of being the most feared and famous man, without rival East or West for his persecution of Christians. Following this claim to worldly supremacy comes a comic scene with his servant which establishes pride in all associated with him. The horse, offstage and suitably fed with oats, is another part of the same argument. He is introduced as:

a palfray,
Ther can no man a better bestryde!
He wyll conducte owur lorde, and gyde
Thorow the world; he ys sure and abyll
To bere a gentyllman. . . . (ll. 122–26)

The wayward Saul then rides out of the first acting area and into the second, the road to Damascus, where, after a further boast, God unseats him, thus overturning the claims for man and beast; and in falling from a horse, Saul falls from the symbol of his own wilfulness. The illustration to Paul's Conversion in MS. Glasgow Gen. 1,111, fol. 47ʳ—a manuscript of Jacobus da Voragine's *Legenda aurea*—adds emphasis by color coding: the horse is decked in brilliant red, the opposite corner is heavenly blue, and Saul/Paul at the moment of his fall/conversion wears both opposing colors (fig. 3). As the Digby play then shows, Saul also falls from being the first among his peers, at the height of his vigor and worldly influence, to being blind, crippled, and needing to be led to the third acting area, where he not only is converted but also becomes the essence of humility.[41] God says to Ananias: "Ther shall ye fynd Saule in humble vyse,/ As a meke lambe that a wolf before was namyd" (ll. 217–18). If, as is also shown in MS. Gen. 1,111, the road to Damascus led up a hill (fig. 3), then the message that Saul falls from all the erring heights associated with the folly of pride would have been further emphasized.[42] However, even without a hill, the staging of Paul's conversion contains a reversal from the negative to the positive understanding of folly. Appropriately, Paul was to be the originator of the observation that the Apostles were "fools for Christ's sake"; therefore his change from arrogance to child-like simplicity would have been particularly pointed. He kneels for his Christening and, though God has chosen him to be a "pynacle of þe fayth" (l. 240), he himself seeks only to be "gydyd and rulyd" (l. 341). Even after his sight is restored he asks Ananias to continue leading him on foot out of the final playing area: "Go forth yowur way," he says, "I wyll succede/ Into what place ye wyll me lede" (ll. 344–45). This is the opposite to the opening where Saul had led the action from the first to the second playing place and had dominated verbally and visually from the highest position on horseback.[43] Homiletic warnings about the horse were frequent enough for this opening use of the animal to bring symbolic readings to mind: as David Jeffrey comments, saint plays were based on sermons and homiletic material.[44]

Further staged metaphors appear in some of the English mystery plays. In Play VIII of the Chester cycle, the Magi enter on horseback and dismount to pray, but it is possible to read kingly error in their conclusions between lines 110 and 112 where they misunderstand the nature of Christ's kingship: "that child would shorten well our waye/ that bringinge presentes to his paye [exchequer],/ and most is of degree."[45] They remount at this point (praising their horses for being dromedaries), and it is possible that the reason they arrive at Herod's palace instead of in the presence of Christ is the fault in their statement, which is subsequently played out on horseback. The stage direction is that they "ryde abowt" (VIII.112 *s.d.*), which indicates confusion and a lengthening rather than a shortening of their way, for their error over the nature of Christ's kingship leads them instead to the fool king. Their mistake is resolved in the subsequent *Merrcers' Playe,* where they discover the reality of Christ's humble birth, between the ox and the ass. Although there is no stage direction, they need to dismount here to give the child the gifts—a practical necessity which involves a lowering of their proud worldly image and expectations. These kings appear to be the mean between two opposing forms of kingship: the heavenly and the diabolical. As representatives of worldly kingship their intentions are good, if inevitably flawed.

In the Towneley *Offering of the Magi,* these kingly figures also enter riding, but error is left entirely with Herod. It is his messenger who intercepts them and obliges them to visit Jerusalem, after which the star disappears because of Herod's anti-Christian influence. To recover their purpose, the kings dismount: "*here lyghtys the kyngys of thare horses*" (XIV.504 *s.d.*) to pray: "*Here knele all þe thre kyngys downe*" (XIV.510 *s.d.*) and immediately the stable is revealed.[46] The scene stages the humility associated with dismounting and, in a way similar to the Chester play, suggests that any discovery of Christ depends more on man's inner state than on his knowledge of geography. It is also in the Towneley plays that the torturers invent a horse-riding punishment in the crucifixion appropriate, as they see it, to Christ's folly of pride:

> Was not this a wonder thyng
> That he durst call hymself a kyng,
> And make so greatt a lee?
> Bot, by Mahowne, whils I may lyf,
> Those prowde wordes shall I neuer forgyf. . . .
> (XXIII.41–45)

The proof that they require is for him to enact his outrageous claim symbolically. He will be seated on a horse—since the cross is wooden, a mock or hobby horse—and once raised in height on "his palfray" (l. 201), the mockery of Christ's assumed folly is completed with the crown of thorns.[47]

But perhaps the most complex use of both ass and horse staging is in the Chester cycle, beginning with the Cappers' play of *Balaam and his ass* (Play V).[48] The play begins with a contrast between King Balack—boasting like a summer fool-king, making warlike and tyrannical gestures from the back of a horse when in fact he proves impotent—and Balaam, on the back of his ass, who is only saved from his own stupidity by the animal's wisdom. Balaam and Balack's servant ride together toward Judea, with the servant also on a horse and Balaam on the ass, thus maintaining a visual contrast between three aspects of foolishness, for the ass persists in saving Balaam in spite of being ill-treated by him[49]—a prefiguration of the concept of Christian folly. In the *Nativity*, which follows, another aspect of worldly folly is included: the "highest horse" (VI. 279) awarded by Octavian to his messenger boy can be read initially as a symbol of the young man's sexual prowess[50] and reflects perhaps Joseph's fears. His response to Mary's pregnancy has been the comic secular one of the old and cuckolded husband:

> And mine yt is not, bee thow bould,
> for I am both ould and could;
> these xxx^{tie} winters, though I would,
> I might not playe noe playe. (VI.133–36)[51]

To Joseph, however, the lad on his high horse symbolizes tyranny: "I wotte by this bosters beere/ that tribute I muste paye" (VI.391–92). After the Chester *Shepherds' Play*, which contains another variant of anti-Christian mock kingship,[52] come the Magi, straying on horseback, then there follows the symbol of Christian folly, sure-footedly carrying the Holy Family into Egypt. In this Chester sequence a matrix is formed through the repeated use of the animals; they present in visual metaphors the contrasts and multiple readings of negative and positive folly, including comic tyranny and Troilus-like lechery in the horse (cf. fig. 4) and in the ass stupidity and innocence with Joseph representing a more secular foolishness since cuckolded husbands were traditionally ridden on donkeys.[53] And it is in the Chester play that Joseph claims the ass is his (X.274). It is possible that part of the conception of the Chester cycle was this continued four-footed manifestation of folly which, as well as having a moral purpose, could also have contributed to the comedy.

The Michel *Passion* does not stage the Nativity, and Gréban made no use of horses in his text. The Valenciennes illustrations too only depict the ass. However, an original antithetical emphasis appears to have been created in *Le Passion de Semur* (c.1500).[54] In Lucifer's revolt in heaven the character of Orgueil enters on horseback to crown him, and since no further use of either animal is made until Christ's entry into Jerusalem, polarized implications are visually reinforced. They are further developed by the detail of the scenes: Orgueil treats heaven as a worldly court—possibly even a court in play—in which he himself is appropriately a chevalier[55] and where Lucifer would be the most appropriate king.

> Honneur soit a la cour joieuse!
> . . .
> Nous . . .
> Vous mectrons en siege real.
> Aidiéz moy, tous levéz amont. [*Pause*]
> Je vous coronne roy du mond,
> De ceans vous dont la matrise. (ll. 287, 294–98)
>
> (All honor to the merry court!
> We will place you in the throne itself.
> Help me—everybody lift.
> I crown you king of the world,
> Over those of whom you are master.)

St. Michael's subsequent call to the good angels contains

the traditional metaphors linking Lucifer's pride to his physical movement upwards: ". . . il ce veul sur Dieu eslever/ Et veul sa chaire hault monter/ Par orgueul et contre raison" ("he wants to raise himself over God and to place his seat high through pride and against reason" [ll. 312–14]).

By contrast, Christ's entry into Jerusalem is, untypically, downwards; he starts the journey from the mountain (*"DEUS debet esse in montem"* [ll. 5478 *s.d.*]) where he reminds his disciples of the humiliation, torture, and death waiting below:

> Nous descendrons dedans Jherusalem
> Ou . . .
>
> . . .
>
> les Juifz le filz de Dieu bailleront
> Aux pecheurs et le condempneront
> De voir a mort.
> Mes tout avant ly bailleront de grans buffes
> . . . de grans reproches et truffes
>
> . . .
>
> Et bien saichés que en la croix morra.
> (ll. 5482–83, 5485–89, 5491)
>
> (We will go down into Jerusalem
> where the Jews will deliver the Son of God
> to sinners and will condemn him to death.
> But beforehand they will submit him to great blows,
> great reproach and mockery . . .
> and it is well known that he will die on the cross.)

He then asks for the ass, the archetypal example of Christian folly, which will lead him to this self-sacrifice. The polarization between pride and humility found in *Legenda aurea* is here played out as a polarization. It is further emphasized in this play further by the fact that Christ's actions are interpreted by the people of Jerusalem as those of a social incompetent. Instead of dwelling on his triumphant reception, as do most other texts, the action moves swiftly to Christ's overturning of the tables in the Temple, where the merchants mock his interruptions as the work of a low-born idiot-depressive:

> Sire, fait il bien le virgine!
> Je vous dix bien, c'est le malvoix.
> Haha! malvoix, malvoix, malvoix,
> Tu est filz de Joseph le fevre
> Et Marie la rouse ta mere.
>
> . . .
>
> Tu es du lignaige Hely.[56]
> (ll. 5671–76, 5678)
>
> (Lord, the virgin's on form!
> I can tell for sure it's old voice-of-doom.
> Ha ha! voice-of-doom, voice-of-doom, voice-of-doom.
> You're the son of Joseph the boilerman
> and red-cheeked Mary.
> You are of holy line.)

Christ persists, and they drive him away with continued mockery of his warnings: "Ha, le grant Dieu! quel pautonier! . . . Va t'am, truant, va hors d'ici!" ("Good God, what a mischief-maker. . . . Push off, beggar, get out of here" [ll. 5689ff]).

The use of the animals in these scenes underlines the antithesis: the image of Lucifer's Orgueil on horseback is that of archetypal satanic folly and, as already noted, that of Christ on the ass archetypal Christian folly, while the scene with the merchants further emphasizes Christ's foolishness or "contemptibility to the world."[57] Omitting the animals from other parts of the play prevents this contrast from becoming obscured.

And it may be possible to find all the above horse and ass associations with folly in the Utrecht illustration (Oxford, Bodleian Library, MS. Douce 93, fol. 34^{v}) of c.1460 showing the Flight into Egypt (fig. 5). In the main picture at the top left of the page, Mary and the Christ Child are seated on an ass, with Joseph attending, while a servant opens the closed circle of the letter out of which the group escapes. In the lower border, bottom right, Herod is on a bay horse on a hillock, watching the slaughter. Herod, the diabolical representative, is dressed as a king or mock king, elevated on combined symbols of pride, the horse and the hill, and juxtaposed against his heavenly opposite. However, Joseph carries a club reminiscent of a fool's bauble, and in view of his ambiguous position, his association with the ass again has suggestions of social foolishness. Further, the servant leading them is bearded, often a sign of dubious morality if not outright folly. Herod too is bearded. The scene he watches is of real cruelty, which might reflect the realities of the hundred years' war, yet the massacre also includes game variants. One woman wields a flail over a soldier, as in some husband and wife flytings (see, for example, Bodleian Library, MS. Hatton 10, fol. 43^r), and another woman appears to be blindfolding another soldier. The acceptability of game-playing in the massacre is no more problematic than that found in plays of Christ's Passion, and this page of illuminations covers the same range of folly found in the Chester cycle —i.e., from Herod's damnable *superbia* in opposition to that needed to save mankind. In between come milder forms of human weakness and festivity, while the concept of antithesis is maintained symbolically through the two animals.

Finally, there are some apparent contradictory uses of them—for example, the horse used in winter Feast of Fools' inversion, when it was given the role of the ass. According to the twelfth-century theologian, Guilelmus Peraldus, it was folly for men to go naked: "like a certain kind of cleric who, in the Feast of Fools, puts his horse in red and himself puts on rushes."[58] It could be that here the horse was simply a substitute for the ass and enjoyed his inversion from low to high, or, more likely, the animal dressed in clerical colors provided satire on the pride of the clergy.

Complementary to this is Nigel de Longchamps' *Speculum Stultorum*, also written in the twelfth century, which provides a more complex reading of the ass. Brunellus' escape at New Year in search of a longer tail, Nigel tells us, portrays the foolishness of a monk or other cleric who "is ambitious for an abbotship or a priorate 'which he might trail behind him like a tail.' . . . The ass's career with its succession of failures ending in disgrace and disappointment is intended to demonstrate the folly of vain pretension and to serve as a warning to the regular clergy."[59] The ass is the obvious symbol for the cleric in the twelfth century because of the *asinaria festa* (fig. 6), but Brunellus' error is to aspire to the ambitious and wilful folly of his more powerful cousin. Troilus, the *cheval fol,* and even Saul in the Digby play of his conversion did temporarily succeed in their misguided aims: part of Brunellus' absurdity is that his ambition is not one he can achieve, and therefore it could be suggested that his pride is less harmful. The ass's folly lies in aspiring to a horse's folly—something that is as absurd as low-born churchmen wishing to emulate secular lords.

Brunellus buys bottles of useless liquid from a mountebank in Salerno which he thinks will extend his tail. His "success" makes him proud, and he boasts, as the Latin says, emptily—*inanis iactantia*—of his noble birth and connection with kings. Immediately after, as he returns to France via Lyon, his boast is punctured. As Mozley's translation puts it, "When fortune smiles how hard it is to see/ The easy fall, the near fatality."[60] The ass takes a short-cut through a field of standing corn (thus giving us the season of midsummer) when Fromund, the Cistercian monk, sets his dogs upon him. The result is that Brunellus loses the rest of the tail he had striven to mend as well as the phials from Salerno; he escapes with his life and nothing else. The foolish boaster in the appropriate season here suffers Fortune's reverses and returns to being the ass he always was. However, it is Fromund the cleric who suffers the more conclusive reversal. Fromund abuses his humble position of monk by his assertion of secular rules of property and power; there are no horse associations, but two bestial comparisons are made. One is a connection between his treachery and that of his hound, Grimbaldus (ll. 1079–81; p. 35), and the second a comparison between his fat girth and that of the ass (l. 883; p. 29). As they walk along the "high bank" of the Rhône (ll. 1063–66; p. 34), Fromund plots Brunellus' death, but the ass makes the first move and "with sudden thrust hurled Fromund from the bank" (l. 1067; p. 34). This brings about a truly fatal reversal, and, interestingly, the description of Fromund's end is the same as that for the later model of the *cheval fol*. The arrogant would-be lord falls from power to immersion in the river, and Brunellus is left to triumph, in this instance more justifiably:

> Sing out, brother asses, high festival hold!
>
> . . .
>
> Sing joyfully, asses, bray out loud and bold,
> With kettle-drum, rattle and gong!
> For . . . Fromund is drowned. (ll. 1075–77, 1081; p. 35)

Cacophony, too, was part of the later *cheval fol* festival. The ass, with his humbler, festive, and basically harmless folly, survives and has the satisfaction of finishing off the perpetrator of the more serious error.[61]

On the surface the horse appears the worthy animal and the ass the worthless, but in these examples their symbolic value is the reverse. The praise of the *Bestiary* becomes dubious since the centaur-like nature of man and horse carries a pejorative meaning in moral works, even implying a less than honorable reality for the noble title of *chevalier*—a title which again derives from a knight's identification with his steed. Whether secular French use of the word could also carry satiric overtones would be the subject of further study, but *chevaliers* were no more immune to satire than were other classes of society.[62] And one twelfth-century fable by Marie de France does suggest that ironic possibilities, linking the horse with the rashness found in Troilus, could also have been perceived in French courtly circles:

> Un cheval vit u herbe crut
> Dedenz un pré, mes n'aparut
> La haie dunt fu clos li prez.

Al saillir enz s'est esteillez.
Ceo funt plusurs, bien le savez:
Tant coveitent lur volentez,
Ne veient pas queile aventure
En vient aprés pesante e dure.[63]

(A horse once saw where grasses grew
In meadowland, but failed to view
The hedge which was the meadow's rim.
He jumped in—thorns impaled him.
You know, with many folks it's thus:
They want a thing so very much
They do not see what consequence,
Heavy and hard, will follow thence.)

NOTES

I am grateful to the British Academy and the Department of Theatre, Film, and Television Studies of Glasgow University for funding which made possible my reading of the original version of this paper at the International Congress on Medieval Studies at Western Michigan University.

[1] *The Bestiary: A Book of Beasts*, trans. T. H. White (1954; rpt. Bath: Alan Sutton, 1992), p. 62, and *Middle English Dictionary* (Ann Arbor: Univ. of Michigan Press, 1959–), *s.v.* 'dog.'

[2] *Bestiary*, trans. White, pp. 84–85.

[3] *Vices and Virtues*, ed. and trans. Ferdinand Holthausen, EETS, o.s. 89 (London: Trübner, 1888), p. 88.

[4] *The Tale of Beryn*, ed. F. J. Furnivall and W. G. Stone, EETS, e.s. 105 (London: K. Paul, Trench, and Trübner, 1909), p. 96 (ll. 3183–84).

[5] *Confessio Amantis*, trans. Terence Tiller (Harmondsworth: Penguin, 1963), p. 229 (VI.1278–82). By the seventeenth century 'bayardly' had come to mean blindly (*OED*).

[6] Quotations from *Troilus and Criseyde* are from *The Riverside Chaucer*, gen. ed. Larry D. Benson (Boston: Houghton Mifflin, 1987).

[7] In the late-thirteenth-century *Renart le nouvel* the bay horse is called "bauchens li senglers" ("with well-strapped girths" [l. 109]), possibly because bay horses were generically hard to control. See *Renart le nouvel par Jacquemart Gielee*, ed. Henri Roussel (Paris: SATF, 1961), p. 17.

[8] Guillaume Paradin, *Mémoires de l'histoire de Lyon* (1573: rpt. Lyon: Éditions Horvath, 1973), pp. 234–35.

[9] Emmanuel Vingtrinier, *La vie Lyonnaise* (Lyon: Bernoux & Cumin, 1898), p. 376. See also François Marie de Fortis, *Voyage pittoresque et historique à Lyon aux environs* (Paris, 1821), pp. 118–20.

[10] This parodies triumphal entries through cities by conquering kings, for whom the upright sword was the symbol of their authority. See Sandra Billington, *Mock Kings in Medieval Society and Renaissance Drama* (Oxford: Clarendon Press, 1991), p. 19.

[11] Vingtrinier, *La vie Lyonnaise*, p. 375, and de Fortis, *Voyage pittoresque et historique*, pp. 118–20. The illustration of 1696 differs from the description attributed to c.1600.

[12] Amable Audin, "Les rites solsticiaux et legende de Saint Pothin," *Revue de l'histoire des religions*, 96 (1927), 161–62.

[13] Quoted in de Fortis, *Voyage pittoresque et historique*, p. 153.

[14] Alciati, however, also expresses admiration for the people's spirit: "Do you wish to know why the region of Thessaly so often changes masters. . . . It does not know how to flatter. . . . But like a high-spirited steed it shakes from its back every groom who does not know how to control it. However, it is not proper for a lord to vent his rage; his only vengeance is to order the beast to suffer a harsher bridle" (trans. Peter M. Daly, *Index Emblematicus*, I [Toronto: Univ. of Toronto Press, 1985], I, No. 35).

[15] *The Adages*, trans. Margaret Mann Philips and R. A. B. Mynors, Collected Works of Erasmus, 31–34 (Toronto: Univ. of Toronto Press, 1982–92), I, 83 (I.vii. 29); IV, 67 (II.viii.47).

[16] *Bestiary*, trans. White, p. 82.

[17] *Old English Homilies and Homiletic Treatises of the Twelfth and Thirteenth Centuries*, 2nd ser.,. ed. and trans. Richard Morris, EETS, o.s. 53 (London: Trübner, 1873), Pt. 2, p. 88. However, several religious works make clear that Jesus chose this "meanest of all beasts."

[18] John Mirk, *Festial*, ed. Theodor Erbe, EETS, e.s. 96 (London: K. Paul, Trench, and Trübner, 1905), p. 251.

[19] *The Ormulum*, ed. Robert Meadows White (Oxford: Oxford Univ. Press, 1852), I, 127–28.

[20] St. Augustine of Hippo, *Sermons for Christmas and Epiphany*, trans. Thomas Comerford Lawler (Westminster, Maryland: Newman Press, 1952), p. 104 (No. 8).

[21] *Cursor Mundi*, ed. Richard Morris, EETS, 62 (London: K. Paul, Trench, and

Trübner, 1875–76), III, 857.

[22] *Vices and Virtues*, trans. Holthausen, p. 92.

[23] *The Ormulum*, I, 127–28 (translation mine).

[24] "Note how exactly the Savior's humility corresponds to the pride of the betrayer. The first man's pride was against God; it went as high as God and even above God. . . . It reached God's height because Adam aspired to divinity. . . . It was above God, as Anselm says, because it willed what God willed that man should not will. . . . But God's son . . . humbled himself . . . his humility reached man's level" (Jacobus de Voragine, *The Golden Legend*, trans. William Granger Ryan (Princeton: Princeton Univ. Press, 1993), I, 42–43.

[25] "When þe kyng of Heuen come þrogh þis ȝeate towart his passyon, he come noþer on hegh hors, ne yn cloþys of gold; but mekely rod on a sympyll asse-backe, leuynge ensampull of mekenes to all crystyn pepull aftyr hym" (Mirk, *Festial*, p. 251).

[26] *Old English Homilies and Homiletic Treatises*, ed. and trans. Richard Morris, EETS, o.s. 29 (London: Trübner, 1868), Pt. 1, p. 4.

[27] *The Chester Mystery Cycle*, ed. R. M. Lumiansky and David Mills, EETS, s.s. 3, 9 (London: Oxford Univ. Press, 1980–86); references in my text are to play and line numbers.

[28] See Augustine, *Sermons for Christmas and Epiphany*, trans. Lawler, p. 121, for the statement that Christ "sent before Him a man, John, to be born at the time when days begin to grow shorter, while He Himself was born when they begin to grow longer. . . . John says: *He must increase, but I must decrease.*"

[29] Ibid., pp. 133–34.

[30] E. K. Chambers, *The Mediaeval Stage* (London: Oxford Univ. Press, 1903), I, 277–78.

[31] Ibid., I, 279n; Margot Fassler, "The Feast of Fools and *Danielis Ludus*: Popular Tradition in a Medieval Cathedral Play," in *Plainsong in the Age of Polyphony*, ed. Thomas Forrest Kelly (Cambridge: Cambridge Univ. Press, 1992), p. 72.

[32] Erasmus, *Adages*, IV, 251–52 (III.ii.71).

[33] Chambers, *The Mediaeval Stage*, I, 286–87. The famous processional *Song of the Ass* in British Library Egerton MS. 2615 is from Beauvais, and occurs immediately prior to the *Ludus Danielis*, which itself has been connected with the reform movement at Beauvais by Fassler, "The Feast of Fools and *Danielus Ludus*," pp. 65–99.

[34] Chambers, *The Mediaeval Stage*, I, 282.

[35] Ibid., I, 298.

[36] See *The Times Whistle* [c.1590], ed. Joseph Meadows Cowper, EETS, o.s. 48 (London: Trübner, 1871), pp. 47–48: "Ruffino, that same roring boy of fame,/ By braules & wenches is diseasde & lame [but buys himself a degree]. . . . Learning was wont to be the highest staire,/ Vpon whose top was fixd preferments chaire/. . . But now the world's altred/ . . . To get preferment who doth now intend,/ He by a golden ladder must ascend;/ . . . paltry pelfe doth worthlesse ignorance/ Vnto the top of learnings mount advaunce" (ll. 1397–1432).

[37] For the four seasons of man's life, see Billington, *Mock Kings*, p. 65.

[38] In a non-satirical vein, Ardennes folklore holds that the whinny of the magical horse Bayard is usually heard on midsummer night (Félix Rousseau, *À travers l'histoire de Namur du Namurois et de la Wallonie*, Collections histoire pro civitate, 46 [Brussels, 1977], pp. 206–07).

[39] On this play see David L. Jeffrey, "English Saints Plays," in *Medieval Drama*, ed. Neville Denny, Stratford-upon-Avon Studies, 16 (London: Edward Arnold, 1973), pp. 82–85, and Clifford Davidson, "The Middle English Saint Play and Its Iconography," in *The Saint Play in Medieval Europe*, Early Drama, Art, and Music, Monograph Ser., 8 (Kalamazoo: Medieval Institute Publications, 1986), pp. 98–105.

[40] *The Late Religious Plays of Bodleian MSS Digby 133 and E Museo 160*, ed. Donald C. Baker, John L. Murphy, and Louis B. Hall, Jr., EETS, 283 (London: Oxford Univ. Press, 1982), p. 1 (*The Conversion of St Paul*, l. 13 *s.d.*). Subsequent references to this play are included in parentheses in my text.

[41] "[L]iterally a fall from pride to humility . . ." (Davidson, "The Middle English Saint Play," p. 102.

[42] Any geographical height, staircase, or hilltop could equate with the top of Fortune's wheel: the highest point of a man's vigor; see Sandra Billington, "Social Disorder, Festive Celebration, and Jean Michel's *Passion JesusCrist*," *Comparative Drama*, 29 (1995), 222. See below for the riverbank.

[43] See Davidson, "The Middle English Saint Play," p. 99, for the necessity of processional movement.

[44] Jeffrey, "English Saints' Plays," p. 83.

[45] In the *Legenda aurea* the kings are not models of virtue: "Chrysostom says that the three kings were called magi because they had been sorcerers but were later converted, and that the Lord chose to reveal his birth to them and to lead them to himself, thereby extending to all sinners the hope of pardon" (*The Golden Legend*, trans. Ryan, I, 79).

[46] *The Towneley Plays*, ed. Martin Stevens and A.C. Cawley, EETS, s.s. 13–14 (London: Oxford Univ. Press, 1994), p. 173; references in my text are to play and

line numbers.

[47] For a different perspective on this iconography, see Rosemary Woolf, "The Theme of Christ the Lover-Knight in Medieval English Literature," *Review of English Studies*, 13 (1962), 1–16.

[48] The horse in the earlier play of *Abraham* has no rider, but the action of Cain pulling his plough could have contained a Bayard reading. Alternatively, and in contrast to the Towneley Cain and Abel (see Richard Axton, *European Drama of the Early Middle Ages* [London: Hutchinson, 1974], pp. 177–78), the Chester Cain play could have used a team of horses, since at least three are needed throughout the cycle. In this case the later Bayard resonances would have been planted with man's first crime. For recent research on Cain's team in the Towneley Cain play, see Margaret Rogerson, "The Medieval Plough Team on Stage: Wordplay and Reality in the Towneley *Mactacio Abel*," *Comparative Drama*, 28 (1994), 182–200.

[49] At this point, or for the whole scene, Balaam's ass is played by a man.

[50] For lustful folly represented by the horse, see Gower, *Confessio Amantis* VII.4995–96; Shakespeare's *Venus and Adonis*, ll. 44–300.

[51] See also V. A. Kolve, *The Play called Corpus Christi* (Stanford: Stanford Univ. Press, 1966), pp. 247–52.

[52] See Billington, *Mock Kings*, pp. 63–71.

[53] See E. P. Thompson, "Rough Music: le charivari anglais," *Annales, économies, sociétées, civilisations*, 28 (1972), 285–312, and Natalie Zemon Davis, *Society and Culture in Early Modern France* (London: Duckworth, 1975), p. 100. Cf. Kolve, *The Play Called Corpus Christi*, pp. 248–49.

[54] *The Passion of Semur*, ed. P. T. Durbin and Lynette Muir, Leeds Medieval Studies, 3 (Leeds:, Univ. Of Leeds Centre for Medieval Studies, 1981).

[55] The word *chevalier* is not used in the Semur *Passion*, but Dame Oyseuse, who rides with him, makes clear she considers him a knight of the best traditions: "Vous . . . me menéz courtoisement. G'iray avec vous voluntiers/ Tous les chemins et les santiers . . ." (ll. 277–83).

[56] See *Dictionnaire historique de l'ancien langage françois*, ed. L. Favré and H. Champion (Niort and Paris, 1880), *s.v.* 'Helie,' from 'Helicon'; also, 'heler' was to drink communally, drinking healths, for which see *Dictionnaire de l'ancienne lange française et de tous ses dialectes du IX*[e] *au XV*[e] *siècle*, ed. Frédéric Godefroy (Paris, 1885).

[57] See *1 Corinthians* 1.28: "ignobilia mundi, et contemptibilia. . . ."

[58] "Ipsi sunt similes cuidam clerico, qui in festo stultorum induit equum scarleto, & ipso indutus erat matta" (Guilelmus Peraldus, *Summa Virtutem ac*

Vitiorum [Moguntiae, 1616], p. 198).

[59] Nigel de Longchamps, *Speculum Stultorum*, ed. John H. Mozley and Robert R. Raymo (Berkeley and Los Angeles: Univ. of California Press, 1960), p. 3; see also Frederic James Edward Raby, *A History of Secular Latin Poetry in the Middle Ages* (Oxford, Clarendon Press, 1934), pp. 94–95.

[60] *A Mirror for Fools: The Book of Burnel the Ass*, trans. John H. Mozley (Notre Dame: Univ. of Notre Dame Press, 1963), p. 28. In my text, page references are to this translation, while line references are to the edition of Mozley and Raymo.

[61] The triumph of the "stupid" animal over the wily could have been adapted from Aesop's Fable of the Wolf and Donkey, which was itself changed in the first printed English version into a moral on the rewards of humility. The donkey's cleverness is removed. See *The Fables of Aesop as First Printed by William Caxton 1484*, ed. Joseph Jacobs (London: David McNutt, 1883), II, 141–43 (Book V, Fable vii).

[62] This is particularly true for the proud anti-heroes of romance literature. See Marie-Luce Chênerie, *Le chevalier errant dans les romans arthuriens en vers des XIIe et XIIIe siècles* (Geneva: Droz, 1986), pp. 378–91, 398.

[63] Marie de France, *Fables*, ed. and trans. Harriet Spiegel (Toronto: Univ. of Toronto Press, 1987), pp. 172–73.

The King His Own Fool: *Robert of Cicyle*

Martin W. Walsh

An important—indeed a vital—document for the study of the medieval court fool is a short "popular" metrical romance entitled *Kyng Robert of Cicyle.* Composed at the end of the fourteenth century in a southeast Midlands dialect, this anonymous poem survives in ten manuscripts, all fairly consistent with each other.[1] This Middle English variant of the motif of the king become his own fool—a "homiletic romance," as Dieter Mehl calls it—is usually considered superior in its story telling to its French source, the *Li dis dou Magnificat*, and its nearest analogue, the German *König im Bade.*[2] The story is this: during evensong the great conqueror and mighty monarch Robert of Sicily takes exception to a verse in the *Magnificat—Deposuit potentes de sede*—and claims that no one can put down *his* power. Falling asleep in his cubicle, he is replaced by an archangel who perfectly assumes his shape and leads the royal retinue out of the chapel. Waking in the dark, Robert shouts for his men but is thereafter treated as a lunatic when he insists that he is indeed the king. He is roughly handled by the palace porter, and, following an interview with the king-angel, he is forced into the role of court fool, an office which he fills for more than three years. Traveling to Rome with the Sicilian court, Robert meets his brothers, Holy Roman Emperor Valamond and Pope Urban, but neither recognizes their kinsman in the ranting fool who claims the throne of Sicily. Nearing the point of despair, Robert meditates upon the fate of Nebuchadnezzar and comes at last to accept his total humiliation. When he can finally admit to the Angel that he is truly a fool, he is secretly restored to his dignities and spends the rest of his days as an ideal monarch, even drafting a memoir of his experience for the edification of his brothers and the world at large.

Brief though it is—scarcely more than five hundred verses—*Kyng Robert of Cicyle* is important with regard to the figure of the court fool in two respects: (1) allowing for the fact that it is a work of fiction, the poem appears accurately to reflect aspects of the historical practice of fool-keeping, and (2) with this as a foundation, the artistic *cum* didactic employment of the court fool motif is sophisticated—one might even venture to say profound.

Regarding actual fool-keeping in the Gothic era, one is impressed by the level of violence in the poem, not only the frustrated violence of the thwarted autocrat but also the casual violence of normal society in its dealings with the *fole* or *wode man*. The Sicilian court is portrayed as a rather elegant, civilized place, and the baiting of the obstreperous loony is never considered "bad" or even particularly unusual behavior.[3] The palace porter, sorely provoked, works over the former king:

Him smot aȝeyn, wiþowten fayle,
Þat neose and mouþ barst a-blood;
Þenne he semed almost wod.
    Þe porter and his men in haste
Kyng Robert in a podel caste;
Vnsemely heo maden his bodi þan,
Þat he nas lyk non oþer man. . . .
(ll. 126–32)

Robert, moreover, is forcibly tonsured:

He heet a barbur him bifore,
Þat as a fool he schulde be schore
Al around, lich a frere,
An honde-brede boue eiþer ere,
And on his croune make a crois.
(ll. 169–73)

Robert's hair is essentially reduced to four symmetrically-placed tufts. We can find rather elaborate examples of the "fool's tonsure" in later art such as the concentric circle pattern on the court fools in the background of a *Crucifixion* by Michael Wohlgemut (1489), in a Luxuria engraving by Meister E. S., in Austrian playing cards of the late fifteenth century, or in the Marriage page of the *Grimaldi Breviary* (c.1520). In a *Crowning with Thorns* panel (1465) by the Colmar master, Gaspard Isenmann, an elegant court fool tips his hat and displays a head shaved into a perfectly symmetrical checker-board pattern.[4] No ass-eared hood or other head gear is mentioned for Robert, nor are the abundant pellet bells of later court fools anywhere in evidence. The tonsure, therefore, must have served as one of the fool's principal attributes in this earlier period—in parody, one would assume, of the symbolic mutilation and humiliation of the professed monastic.

In the version edited by Hazlitt, Robert is also given a *babulle*. This is not described but might well have comprised a fool's head on the end of a baton as is frequently encountered in the visual arts from the late thirteenth century onward. Earlier fools in manuscript illuminations have as their mock scepter simply a long club or a stick with attached bladder for administering soft beatings. The *Oxford English Dictionary* cites *Kyng Robert* as the earliest instance of the word 'bauble' meaning the fool-headed staff. An example of the nearly naked fool with both tonsure and the bauble is present in a mid fourteenth-century French psalter in the Bodleian Library (MS. Douce 211, fol. 258v; see fig. 7).[5]

Multiplication of the fool's ridiculous image is certainly intended in Robert's case, whether or not he bears the more elaborate bauble, for he is also joined with an *ape* (or monkey), which the Angel will dress exactly like him: "I schal him cloþen as þi broþer/ Of o cloþing . . ." (ll. 159–60).[6] Robert's costume is later described as a "lodly garnement,/ Wiþ ffoxes tayles mony aboute" (ll. 248–49) such as we find on the Carnival cripples in Bruegel a century and a half later.[7] The foxtail would be fairly common in later fool iconography, especially in German Carnival plays and satirical broadsheets of the sixteenth and seventeenth centuries—e.g., in Hans Sachs' *Fuchsschwanz-kram* (*Foxtail Market*). Arlecchino of the *commedia dell'arte* would also occasionally sport one. The dwarf-fool Godfrey Gobelyve in Stephen Hawes' *Passetyme of Pleasure* (1505) is outfitted "With a hood, a bell, a foxtayle and a bagge."[8] The foxtail as hand prop appears to be an alternative to the bladder for flogging purposes. To be whipped with a foxtail clearly signified being flouted by a jester figure. Wearing several foxtails on one's garment, however, might well have other meanings—e.g., marking the wearer as "vermin" to be "hunted." Robert's costume, it is clear, does not serve a decorative function as do the garments of the bright particolored fools often seen capering about at banquets or jousts in the illuminations of calendar pages or tournament books of subsequent centuries. Robert's "loathsome garment" is presumably a peasant's tunic or cloak decorated only as a means of enhancing his marginality. Robert began his second career dirty and wet with a bloody nose and mouth, and his subsequent investiture does not improve his appearance for court service but rather renders him more permanently grotesque.

Robert's "conditioning" for the job of court fool is treated at some length by the poet, who returns to the subject several times in the course of the tale. Robert must eat from one dish with the "houndes þat beþ in halle" (l. 203). At first he refuses thus to debase himself, but hunger and thirst eventually drive him to compete for the scraps commonly thrown to the pets in the course of a meal in the hall. This is apparently the only way Robert is nourished for the three years and more of his tenure as court fool. Henry VIII's fool, Will Sommers, was famous for sleeping with the royal spaniels, but Robert's case seems the more extreme.[9]

The "entertainment" Robert provides the court is similarly one-dimensional like that of a pet animal: no song, music, dance, witty banter, or even innocent babble, but simply the delusional rantings of a psychotic. The angel-king makes a point of quizzing Robert every day concerning his identity, and every day Robert roars out his absurd claims, much to the cruel glee of the entourage: "Þer nas in court grom ne page/ Þat of þe Kyng ne made rage" (ll. 189–90). The Angel himself is not above ironic word-play at his expense. When Robert vows that his powerful brothers will revenge him to the full, the Angel replies, "That semyth the wele," but "The crowne semyth the no thyng welle" (ed. Hazlitt, ll. 255–56); this may be translated as "So it appears to you, but the crown becomes you not." Earlier, the Angel had fully established Robert as a mock king. His *ape* will serve as his councillor from whom he might learn wisdom. Even more ironically, Robert is assigned a royal taster: "Þin assayour schal ben an hound,/ To assaye þi mete bifore þe" (ll. 166–67). Robert's madness is all too apparent (*wode* is the most frequent adjective applied to him), and it is this "routine" of insisting on his royal status alone which earns him his place as court fool. It is interesting that such "delusions of grandeur" were already recognized at this early date as a shorthand for incurable madness, and in this regard Robert anticipated the naked monarch in the final Bedlam scene of Hogarth's *Rake's Progress* or the obligatory Napoleon in a vaudeville nut-house sketch. Among historical fools, we might also mention that member of Elizabeth I's household who bore the ironic name "Monarcho."[10]

The starkness, indeed the cruelty of this portrait of the court fool has, I believe, the ring of truth about it. The depiction of the fool here is closer to fact than to fiction and certainly does not prettify or sentimentalize the figure. There is not space here to explore all of the comparative material gathered by Karl Friedrich Flögel, Dr. Doran, Alfred Canel, Enid Welsford, Barbara Swain, and, more recently, Maurice Lever and Sandra Billington on historical court fools who were mentally defective or mentally disturbed.[11] Suffice it to say that the poem of *Robert of Cicyle* gives not only one of the most complete pictures of the treatment of such a "natural" but also one of the earliest.

Details of Robert's accouterment are corroborated by contemporary visual arts and by later folk practice (as with Brueghel's cripples), though in the later centuries the fool's props and costume took a decided turn toward the decorative, even the pretty, as Humanist interest in the type ameliorated to some degree the harsher medieval view of the "bare forked animal," the fool who sayeth in his heart, "There is no God" of the psalmist, or the fool who proveth by his actions that man is little better than a beast.

The poem, of course, is not reportage but *teaching*. The point is not to feel pity for fools as a class but to endorse the fact that Robert deserves everything he gets—an indirect argument for the essential realism of the court background. How could an audience believe in Robert's punishment if his penance was well beyond their experience? The poet everywhere wishes to maximize the distance of Robert's prideful fall:

For he wende in none wyse
þat God Almihti couþe deuyse
Him to bringe to lower stat;—
Wiþ o drauht he was chekmat!

. . .

He was defygured in a þrowe,
So lowe er þat was neuer kyng;
Allas, her was a deolful þing,
Þat him scholde for his pryde
Such hap among his men betyde!
(ll. 181–84, 192–96)

Robert is the inevitable "loser" in his prideful match with God. He is consistently reminded throughout that his status now is that of *vnderlyng*, one of the most common terms applied to him along with *gadelyng*, *harlot*, and of course *fol*.

Robert's fall and eventual recovery are carefully contextualized in the ceremonial calendar. The fateful evensong is "a Seynt Iones Niht" (l. 29)—that is, on Midsummer Eve, recognized as a time for the intersecting of realms long before Shakespeare's *Midsummer Night's Dream*—e.g., in Dunbar's *Tretis of the Twa Marrit Wemen and the Wendo.* The *Magnificat* verse, on the other hand, is of paramount importance to a different festive period. *Deposuit potentes de sede/ Et exaltavit humiles* provided the opportunity and the "authority" for the lower cathedral clergy of the High Middle Ages to celebrate their great festival of inversion, the *Festa asinorum* or *stultorum,* during the Christmas-to-Epiphany season. The poet quite deliberately intersects Midsummer with its calendar opposite, Christmastide—a point made by Billington in her *Mock Kings in Medieval Society and Renaissance Drama.*[12] In Robert's case it is not carnivalesque liberation that he experiences but rather traumatic imprisonment in the role of fool. And instead of a stimulating encounter with Faerie, that perennial and desirable Other, Robert is caught in a mirror of his own devising. During the three-year period of his trial, it will be recalled, Robert continually confronts a perfect simulacrum of himself as king—a figure who, moreover, ideally fills the role-model which Robert, otherwise a paragon, had seriously compromised with his arrogance and ire:

> Þe angel was kyng, him þhouȝte long;
> In his tyme was neuer wrong,
> Tricherie, ne falshede, ne no gyle
> Idon in þe lond of Cisyle.
> Alle goode þer was gret plenté:
> Among men loue and charité;
> In his tyme was neuer strif
> Bitwene mon and his wyf;
> Vche mon louede wel oþer:
> Beter loue nas neuere of broþer.
> Þenne was þat a ioyful þing
> In londe to haue such a kyng.
> (ll. 207–18)

The shining realm of Faerie is here made a poltical reality under the angelic monarch. The utopian suspension of time in a Golden Age, characteristic of both carnivalesque festival and intersections with Faerie, are turned rather skillfully toward the larger didactic purpose. Robert's sleep at evensong opens onto a permanent "bad dream." But unlike Calderón's Sigismundo in *La vida es sueño* who is shut away in darkness, King Robert inhabits a perfectly familiar world, his own court of Sicily, where, however, he experiences the maximum in role reversal.

The usurper king, moreover, presents a picture of dazzling radiance as if his angelic nature were beginning to shine through the disguise. On his entry into Rome the Angel is clad in snow white garments set with an abundance of pearls. He dispenses gifts of clothing made of fabrics which seem of unearthly origin. In his splendid entourage, "Of cloþus, gurdeles, and oþer þing,/ Eueriche sqyȝer [was] þhouȝte a kyng" (ll. 264–65).

As the king begins to manifest himself as Angel-on-Earth, Robert reaches the depths of degradation. He had long been depending upon his brothers to revenge him on this strange usurper in his own image. The movement toward his restoration begins with an invitation from his brother the Emperor to join him that they might both travel to their "brother" the Pope for splendid celebrations "In Roome an Holy Þoresday" (l. 232). Robert reaches his nadir when his own flesh and blood fail to recognize him and when indeed they join in the fun against him. It is not by accident that it is Passion week. Without directly summoning up the image of the "Man of Sorrows," the poet does move Robert into a deep penitential mode through a long rumination on the fate of King Nebuchadnezzar. The three royal brothers, like some high earthly model of the Trinity, celebrate together for five weeks—that is, through the entire Easter season. Very soon after, the Angel restores Robert and returns to heaven in the "twynklyng of an eȝe." The date is, we may understand, near or actually on the feast of the Ascension. There is not a precise one-for-one correlation with the liturgical calendar—rather this is suggested as a backdrop to the story—but Robert's final repentance and realization of his position as Fool *vis-à-vis* the Godhead is rather subtly grounded.

The Nebuchadnezzar meditation, taking up some

seventy lines, refers to a legendary accretion based on the account in the fourth chapter of the book of *Daniel* which I am so far unable to trace. According to our poet, *Nabugodonosor* fell into madness from grief over the death of one of his favorite knights, *Sire Olyferne,* who had often flattered him with the "name of God." This figure could be the Assyrian general Holofernes introduced from the *Apocrypha*. In our poem, however, he is simply "slaye in hard schour" (l. 324) with no mention of the avenging hand of Judith. In any case, the biblical lesson remains central. Nebuchadnezzar for his presumption of divine powers runs mad in the desert: "Fyftene ȝer he liuede þare,/ With rootes, gras, and euel fare" (ll. 327–28). Robert directly identifies with him: "Nou am i in such caas,/ And wel worse þen he was" (ll. 333–34). Through this complete identification Robert comes to a new faith and hope in God's mercy. Robert accepts the fact that he must "leve so here for evyrmore,/ As levyd Nabegodhonosore" (ed. Hazlitt, ll. 410–11) and re-enacts the biblical king's conversion. He points to the exemplum of the fallen angels and rises to a confession and *miserere* of genuine pathos and intensity:

Lord, on þi fool þow haue pité!
I hedde an errour in myn herte,
And þat errour doþ me smerte;
Lord, i leeued not on þe.
On þi fol þou haue pité!
Holy Writ i hedde in dispyt;
For þat is reued my delyt—
For þat is riht a fool i be!
Lord, on þi fool þou haue pité!
Lord, i am þi creature;
Þis wo is riht þat i dure,
And wel more, ȝif hit may be.
Lord, on þi fool þou haue pité!
Lord, i haue igult þe sore! *sinned against*
Merci, Lord: i nul no more;
Euere þi fol, Lord, wol i be.
Lord, on þi fol [þou] haue pité.
(ll. 348-64)

Robert also calls upon *Blisful Marie,* thus looping us back to the *Magnificat* whose verse he had held in such contempt. Robert's essential ignorance was underscored very early by the fact that "in Latyn he nuste what heo songe" (l. 38) and needed indeed to have the *Deposiuit* verse translated for him before he could dismiss it. This was the first and defining act of folly. In this culminating monologue Robert runs the gamut of medieval fool images from the beastly wildman—"al of mos his cloþing was" (l. 329)—to the Pauline fool-in-Christ or fool-for-Christ's-sake —"wrech of wrechys men me calle,/ And fole of alle foles" (ed. Hazlitt, ll. 397–98).[13] Having reached this point of illumination, Robert's restoration is guaranteed. He then can pass his final examination with flying colors:

> "What artou?" seide þe angel.
> "Sire, a fol; þat wot i wel,
> And more þen fol, ȝif hit may be;
> Kep i non oþer dignité."
> (ll. 389–92)

Robert is restored to his throne, and the court behaves towards him as if nothing unusual had occurred. All is not "happily ever after," however, for Robert has only some two years left to live. Evidently his experience as fool had broken him physically. He does live as a pious, charitable king, but his principal work is to commit his story to writing and to disseminate it through his brothers to the world. There is thus an interesting metatextual touch here at the end, for Robert's memoir is, of course, the poem we have just experienced.

If one were to characterize the employment of the fool image in *Kyng Robert,* one might call it an essentially Franciscan rather than a proto-Humanist one, for in it is reflected not the attitude of Erasmus assuming the voice of *Moria* herself but of Ramón Llull giving the idiotic court fool in his *Blanquerna* his own name: Ramón.[14] The *Kyng Robert* poem is grounded in a general verisimilitude, as is here argued, demonstrating a simple but workmanlike construction and a tight focus, and so achieves both power and immediacy in its moral teaching. It is indeed a romance raised to the level of a sermon.

I would like to make one final observation on this rather accomplished Middle English employment of the fool motif. *Robert of Cicyle* was such a popular tale that it was dramatized on at least three occasions in the following century and a half—at Lincoln in 1481–82, at Chester in 1531, and at the Jesuit college in St. Omer in 1623—although all of these play texts are lost.[15] If we had them, we would no doubt encounter a theatrical court fool of far greater complexity than the usual capering Vices of fifteenth-century moralities (fool as sinner, pure and simple) or the witty, often musical jester reflecting the Humanist topos of "all are Fools in the great *theatrum mundi*." It would be a stage fool that looks forward not to marginal grotesques and entertainers but to title roles, to the heart of the English dramatic achievement, to Richard II, Hamlet, and Lear.[16]

NOTES

[1] For commentary and bibliography, see J. Burke Severs, ed., *A Manual of the Writings in Middle English, 1050–1500* (New Haven: Connecticut Academy of Art and Sciences, 1967), I, 171–72, 330–32. See also Lilian Herlands Hornstein, "*King Robert of Sicily:* A New Manuscript," *PMLA*, 78 (1963), 453–58. Quotations in my article are from *Middle English Metrical Romances*, ed. Walter Hoyt French and Charles Brockway Hale (1930; rpt. New York: Russell and Russell, 1964), II, 933–46, which reproduces the text in the Vernon manuscript (Bodleian Library, MS. English Poetry A.1, fols. 330ff). Reference is also made in my article to the transcription of Cambridge University Library MS. Ff.2.38 (conflated with a Harleian manuscript) by W. Carew Hazlitt, *Remains of the Early Popular Poetry of England* (London: John Russell Smith, 1864), I, 264–88.

[2] Dieter Mehl, *The Middle English Romances of the Thirteenth and Fourteenth Centuries* (New York: Barnes and Noble, 1969), pp. 124–25. See also Laura A. Hibbard, *Mediaeval Romance in England* (New York: Oxford Univ. Press, 1924), pp. 58–64; Lilian Herlands Hornstein, "*King Robert of Sicily*: Analogues and Origins," *PMLA*, 79 (1964), 13–21; and Alexandra Hennessey Olsen, "The Return of the King: A Reconsideration of *Robert of Sicily* ," *Folklore*, 93 (1982), 216–19.

[3] The poem certainly means to evoke the golden age of Norman Sicily

(eleventh to twelfth centuries). Its historicity is only generally accurate, however. The historical kings of Sicily, Roger I (1031–1101) and Roger II (1093–1154), seem to have been conflated with Robert the Devil, Duke of Normandy. And while a famous Pope Urban can be found in the period—Urban II (c.1042–99), preacher of the First Crusade—an Emperor Valamond his brother cannot. Whether this late fourteenth-century English poem was understood to reflect as well upon the prideful Richard II is an interesting matter for speculation.

[4] Werner Mezger, *Narrenidee und Fastnachtsbrauch* (Constance: Universitätsverlag Konstanz, 1991), pp. 85, 227–31, 459. See also E. Tietze-Conrat, *Dwarves and Jesters in Art* (New York: Phaidon, 1957), fig. 65. The Isenmann panel is in the Musée d'Unterlinden, Colmar. Cf. Francis Douce, "On the Clowns and Fools of Shakespeare," in *Illustrations of Shakespeare and of Ancient Manners* (London, 1839), Pl. II.

[5] D. J. Gifford, "Iconographical Notes towards a Definition of the Medieval Fool," *Journal of the Warburg and Courtauld Institutes*, 37 (1974), 336–42. See also Hadumoth Meier, "Die Figur des Narren in der christlichen Ikonogaphie des Mittelalters," *Das Münster*, 8 (1955), 1–11.

[6] See H. W. Janson, *Apes and Ape Lore* (London: Warburg Institute, 1952), esp. chap. 7; Robert of Sicily is cited on p. 211.

[7] Brueghel, *The Beggars* (1568), Musée du Louvre, Paris. A similar group was included in the famous *Combat of Carnival and Lent* (1559), Kunsthistorisches Museum, Vienna.

[8] Stephen Hawes, *Passetyme of Pleasure*, as quoted in Enid Welsford, *The Fool: His Social and Literary History* (New York: Farrar and Rinehart, 1935), pp. 72, 123, 190, 291. See also Mezger, *Narrenidee und Fastnachtsbrauch*, pp. 258–68.

[9] See *A Shakespeare Jestbook: Robert Armin's* Foole upon Foole *(1600)*, ed. James Hogg (Salzburg: Institut für Englische Sprache und Literatur, Universität Salzburg, 1973), p. 128.

[10] Welsford, *The Fool*, p. 170.

[11] Karl Friedrich Flögel, *Geschichte der Hofnarren* (Leipzig, 1789); [John] Doran, *The History of Court Fools* (London: Richard Benley, 1858); Alfred Canel, *Recherches historiques sur les fous des Rois de France* (Paris, 1873); Barbara Swain, *Fools and Folly during the Middle Ages and Renaissance* (New York: Columbia Univ. Press, 1932); Maurice Lever, *Le sceptre et la marotte* (Paris: Artheme Fayard, 1983); Sandra Billington, *A Social History of the Fool* (New York: St. Martin's Press, 1984).

[12] Sandra Billington, *Mock Kings in Medieval Society and Renaissance Drama* (Oxford: Clarendon Press, 1991), p. 91.

[13] For the equation of mad Nebuchadnezzar with the legendary wildman, see Timothy Husband, *The Wild Man: Medieval Myth and Symbol* (New York: Metropolitan Museum of Art, 1980), pp. 8–10.

[14] Ramón Llull, *Blanquerna*, ed. and trans. E. A. Peters and Robert Irwin (London: Dedalus, n.d.), chap. lxxix.

[15] See my "Looking in on a Lost Drama: The Case of *King Robert of Sicily*," *Fifteenth-Century Studies*, 14 (1988), 191–201. The dramatic viability of the extant poem was recently tested by the University of Michigan's Harlotry Players in an experimental performance under the author's direction. Through a combination of recitation, dumb-show, and actual "scenes" the Middle English poem proved, with only minor editing, to be quite stageworthy. Performances were between February and May 1995 at the University of Michigan Art Museum; at the Twenty-fifth Center for Medieval and Renaissance Studies Conference, Ohio State University; and at the Thirtieth International Congress on Medieval Studies, Western Michigan University.

[16] See also John Wasson, "The Secular Saint Plays of the Elizabethan Era," in *The Saint Play in Medieval Europe*, ed. Clifford Davidson, Early Drama, Art, and Music, Monograph Ser., 8 (Kalamazoo: Medieval Institute Publications, 1986), pp. 255–57.

Forgotten Fools: Alexander Barclay's *Ship of Fools*

Robert C. Evans

By definition, fools are different: they diverge from what is common, whether it be common sense, common judgment, or even common morality. They are outsiders, embodiments of "the Other," and, for that reason, the way a culture reacts to its fools can tell us much about that culture itself. Willingly or not, fools violate custom or convention; they transgress, and their very designation as "fools" can function as punishment, warning, or sometimes even praise. Fools are important, therefore, precisely because they are perceived as outsiders: a culture partly defines itself by defining its fools. For all these reasons, studying fools seems oddly wise.

Like any marginal group, fools highlight (by contrast) a culture's deepest values, its core assumptions. Or, rather, they expose a culture's fault-lines, its points of conflict and contention. Because no culture is likely to agree (with absolute unanimity) in its definition of foolishness, the ways in which fools are defined—by different groups and for different purposes—are therefore essentially *political* acts, part of an on-going struggle for power. To speak of "a culture," indeed, is misleadingly static and monolithic. "A culture" is composed of sub-cultures and coalitions, constantly in motion and conflict, and the struggle to define the category of "fools" is simply one of the most revealing ways these conflicts reveal themselves. Studying fools, then, can help expose not only what holds a "culture" together but also what threatens to tear it apart. Thus the struggle to define a set of fools (even wise fools, like Lear's) is inevitably a struggle to define (and impose) core values. Defining fools is a serious matter indeed.

In our efforts to explain the connections and distinctions between the Middle Ages and the Renaissance, therefore, it might be especially helpful to examine the ways these eras defined their fools. And in examining that issue, it seems especially useful to turn to one of the most important texts of a highly important transitional period. Scholars who have studied Sebastian Brant's *Narrenschiff*, or *Ship of Fools*, call it one of the most widely read and widely influential books of the Renaissance. Its impact was even greater in France than in Germany, and even greater still in England than in Germany or France.[1] The book was one of the first truly international best-sellers at the beginning of the age of print, and it has been called "one of the most successful books recorded in the whole history of literature."[2] On average, a new edition has appeared every six years for the last 450 years,[3] but the book's first reception, following its publication in 1494, is even more impressive. F. H. Jamieson notes that it was quickly "translated into the leading languages of Europe at a time when translations of new works were only the result of the most signal merits," so that "its success was then quite unparalleled."[4] Versions soon appeared in Low German, Dutch, and Flemish, with two in Latin, three in French, and two in English.[5] These many versions were often reprinted and frequently pirated, and the original was variously expanded, altered, and adapted to suit readers of different lands, languages, and backgrounds. John Van Cleve has called the initial response "sustained and unprecedented," while an earlier writer termed the book a "secular Bible which nourished an entire age."[6]

Given this enormous impact, it seems all the more surprising that the sixteenth-century English versions have attracted such little attention. Even the *Narrenschiff* itself has not been much discussed in recent English-language scholarship, and a check of the 1981–94 MLA computerized bibliography, for instance, turned up only one brief entry (in a Japanese periodical) on the *Ship of Fools*, although 209 items dealt with "fools."[7] Almost nothing has appeared for centuries on Henry Watson's 1509 version in English prose, which was never reprinted after 1517. The situation is a little better concerning Alexander Barclay's famous (but often neglected) translation, also issued in 1509 and then republished in 1570. Scholars who have looked at Barclay usually concede his importance, but few have looked and fewer still have lingered. Studies of Barclay's *Ship of Fools* are increasingly rare, and a fine recent overview of sixteenth-century literature mentions him only twice in passing, each time dismissively (and once with an incorrect first name).[8] The chief purposes of this essay, then, are to survey the history of past scholarship dealing with Brant and Barclay; to provide an overview of the most recent work; and to suggest how the insights generated by students of Brant might usefully be applied to Barclay. Finally, in an appendix, I will argue for the importance of preparing a new scholarly edition of Barclay's *Ship of Fools*. Barclay quite simply has major importance for our study of a crucial historical period, and for the full significance of his *Ship* to be recognized we will require a more readable and accurate text than has been available hitherto.

The recent neglect of Barclay seems surprising in view of his impact during the Renaissance itself. In 1886, for instance, C. H. Herford claimed that Barclay's was the only English book of its day to enjoy "the privilege of being read for nearly a century after it was written."[9] Although later scholars have sometimes questioned certain of Herford's other assertions,[10] Barclay's influence seems undeniable, if largely unexplored. R. M. Alden, for example, called the *Ship of Fools* "the most important work in the history of English satire before the Elizabethan period" and asserted that it contains the first use of the word 'satire' in all the English works he surveyed.[11] In addition, Arthur Koebling and other scholars see the *Ship of Fools* as a key influence not only on later satire but also on Elizabethan emblem literature.[12] Moreover, the work's influence on drama has been frequently asserted if not always fully demonstrated.[13] David Carlson, in a fine recent overview, contends that Barclay was "the only native writer of the early Tudor period whose works went immediately and regularly into the wide and comparatively popular circulation that print afforded," and he also notes that Barclay "was one of the first English writers to be honored with the [posthumous] publication of an edition of his complete (or nearly complete) works."[14] James A. S. McPeek claims that Barclay's *Ship of Fools* was "deeply influential in English literature of the Renaissance," and in fact Edwin Zeydel declares that Brant's impact in England was "ascribable wholly to Barclay's and Watson's translations and to French imitations of Brant."[15] The German *Narrenschiff* seems to have been little read in Britain—a fact that increases the significance of Barclay's translation.

Indeed, the term 'translation' is misleading, since Barclay freely expanded, altered, and adapted his mainly French and Latin sources, which were themselves hardly faithful to Brant's German. Thus the vitality of the *Ship of Fools* is indicated not only by how often it was translated but also by how often it was transformed; Barclay and the others saw themselves less as imitators than as emulators, trying to achieve effects comparable (but not identical) to those achieved by Brant. Barclay's version probably owed its impact to many factors. David R. Anderson, for instance, in a dissertation that offers a superb (but unpublished) overview, notes that Barclay's book was the first volume printed in England to use the Roman typeface favored by Renaissance humanists.[16] Hence a book that today seems old-fashioned would at first have seemed trendy. The fact that Barclay's *Ship of Fools* juxtaposed the Latin text (in Roman type) with the English text (in Gothic or "black letter" type) would have given the book both scholarly prestige and popular appeal, and the fact that both the Latin and the English were so heavily annotated with classical and biblical citations would have confirmed that this was a serious work, however merely humorous its text and woodcuts might appear.

The woodcuts, of course, contributed enormously to the work's appeal.[17] They were one of the most innovative aspects of a book whose themes were largely traditional, and indeed it has been suggested that the cuts made even poor translations not only palatable but also popular.[18] Although the woodcuts in Barclay's version were not exact copies of the ones in Brant and are usually considered inferior, they obviously added extra interest to the text.[19] C. H. Herford commented, for example, that "the somewhat hesitating and precarious dramatic life" of the poetry "is powerfully enforced by the invariably vivid woodcuts. When the description is most formal and abstract, or loses itself in parallels and 'examples,' the auxiliary art silently secures that the poet shall not be talked out by the moralist."[20] The same point has been made about Brant's text, which Helmut Rosenfeld considers a contribution to early journalism.[21] Yet we should not over-emphasize the woodcuts as the decisive factor in work's appeal. Jamieson rejects the idea that the woodcuts alone accounted for Brant's popularity,[22] and his argument is strongly supported by Patricia Gillis' demonstration that most editions of Brant published after 1520 omitted the cuts—firm evidence of the popularity of the poem itself.[23] Thus, although Thomas Cramer plausibly sees the *Ship of Fools* as highly innovative in its tight integration of the visual and verbal arts,[24] we should never simply assume that the pictures overshadowed the text.

In fact, no simple explanation of the popularity or influence of the *Ship of Fools* can be offered or accepted. Centuries of analysis and scholarship have yielded numerous, even contradictory explanations, no one of which seems satisfactory in itself. The mere existence of so many different theories implies the rich suggestiveness of the *Ship of Fools*, the many ways it may have appealed to many diverse kinds of readers. The *Ship of Fools* still lends itself to different points of view and must have done so from the start, although very few of these viewpoints have been brought to bear specifically on Barclay. Applying to Barclay the insights already offered by scholars of Brant might help illuminate each writer's distinctive achievements, contexts, and points of view. Surprisingly, although scholarship on Brant epitomizes all the major debates of modern studies of the period, few of its findings have yet been tested on Barclay.

Some scholars, for instance, have seen Brant's *Ship of Fools* as profoundly conservative and medieval, while others have stressed its religious, social, philosophical, and especially humanistic innovations. Patricia Gillis, for instance, quotes the historian Henry Charles Lea, writing in the canonical *Cambridge Modern History*, who argues:

> There was no product of humanistic literature . . . which so aided in paving the way for the Reformation as the *Narrenschiff*, . . . [in which] the Church is never referred to as the means through which the pardon of sin and the grace of God are to be obtained. . . . The lesson is taught that man deals directly with God and is responsible to Him alone. . . .[25]

Similarly, Hans-Georg Kemper argued (as summarized by John Van Cleve in his book-length overview of Brant criticism) that Brant's modernistic ethical system "is no longer solely orthodox Christian but in part rational and secular."[26] Likewise, Anton Zijderveld contends that Brant's effectiveness was partly due to the fact (as Zijderveld sees it)

> that he did not employ any theological arguments, as such arguments had lost much of their former authority. He did not, as some have claimed, belong to the pre-Reformation movement of protest against Rome. He remained a loyal, rather conservative member of the Roman Church, although there is not a shred of religious devotion in his book. On the contrary, the attentive reader discovers between the deceptively primitive lines of his vernacular German, thoughts and ideas which are remarkably rationalistic. . . . Folly is now equated with human weakness which can be cured by man himself through his becoming ever more rational.[27]

Similarly, Van Cleve paraphrases Bernhard Ohse's view that the *Ship of Fools* "is anything but a compendium of theological statements. Brant's first concern lies with the correction of unethical behavior without recourse to elaborate theological argumentation."[28] Van Cleve also summarizes Barbara Könneker's claim that "Brant's contribution to the new *Geist* was his insistence on the application of reason, on a common-sense ethics, and on an ascetic individualism."[29] According to Van Cleve, Friedrich Zarncke saw the *Ship of Fools* as the "first literary result of the tension between a high medieval, feudal ethos and a late medieval, bourgeois ethos."[30] Zijderveld offers a similar view, arguing that Brant depicts the fool as "someone who does not know how to behave himself correctly," while depicting the wise person as one "who contains his emotions and adjusts his behavior to the predominant bourgeois norms and values."[31] According to Van Cleve, Helmut Rosenfeld also sees the *Ship of Fools* as "representative of the decline of social consciousness among writers and the rise of a perception of individual responsibility."[32] How many (if any) of these ideas are relevant to Barclay's version and its impact in England is a topic that needs to be much more fully explored.

Unlike scholars who see the *Ship of Fools* as heralding a sea-change in ethics, religion, and social values, others see the work as profoundly conservative. Van Cleve summarizes Robert Weimann, for instance, as arguing that Brant's view of individualism is "conservative and medieval, because the one who is isolated and who isolates himself is the fool."[33] Although Kenneth J. Northcott is summarized as arguing that even Brant's conservatism is bourgeois, since "the poet mocks peasants not for being ignorant but for aspiring to be burghers," East German Marxists contended that Brant's ideology is retrogressive, offering "a skeptical, conservative analysis of society that duly attacks ethical abuses but remains blind to progressive developments."[34] Indeed, Van Cleve notes that Helmut Birkhan investigated Brant's debts to the medieval satirical tradition, and David Anderson's view that Barclay's version is even more medieval than Brant's[35] is supported by G. R. Owst's emphasis on parallels between Barclay's text and medieval sermons.[36] For Barbara Swain, Brant's view is that following order "is the essence of wisdom. Brant's whole literary purpose was to teach obedience to the law of God and compliance with the code of man," and she contends that both Brant and Barclay "look to the established order, rather than to change, for help."[37] The same point is more positively made by Patricia Gillis. Unlike Zijderveld (who claims that Brant deemphasizes Christ as redeemer[38]), Gillis contends that the *Ship of Fools* is strongly religious and extremely orthodox. As she puts it, "Brant is on all points in perfect agreement with the teachings of the Church. . . . [T]he basic assumption of the necessity of grace and of the Church as its vessel underlies his poem from beginning to end."[39] Even when he attacks churchmen, "it is never for error but always for corruption; he aims at restoration and purification so that Holy Church can perform her ministry effectively."[40] To what degree are any of these claims true? And, in particular, to what degree are they true for Barclay? Once again, these are topics that remain to be much more fully explored. They have only been touched on in the tiny body of criticism dealing specifically with Barclay's work.

Not only questions of theme, meaning, and intellectual context, however, deserve our fuller attention when we try to assess the impact of Brant and especially of Barclay. Questions of style, genre, and technique are also very important. As noted above, part of the influence of the *Ship of Fools* must have been due to its attractive format, especially the woodcuts, but scholars have also offered other explanations for the work's aesthetic and literary appeal. According to Anderson, for instance, it is important to recognize that the *Ship of Fools* set sail at the start of the great period of emblem literature.[41] Although scholars have debated whether the *Ship of Fools* can precisely be called emblematic, the basic similarities seem fairly obvious and have been explored by such writers as Barbara Tiemann, C. H. Herford, Barbara Swain, and Holger Homann.[42] Indeed, David Anderson has argued that Barclay's version resembles later emblems even more strongly than Brant's, since Barclay provides a verse "motto" along with a Latin title and summary to accompany the picture and the main text.[43] Ironically, the fact that the generally cruder cuts in Barclay are less finely detailed than their German originals makes them, Anderson argues, even more emblematic by emphasizing their "non-realistic, symbolic quality."[44] The favorable reception of the *Ship of Fools* must have been affected by the same mentality that nurtured the popularity of emblems, and indeed the reprinting of Barclay in 1570 seems to have been spurred by the recent publication of Jan van der Noot's emblematic *Theatre for Worldlings*.[45]

Another factor that seems to have promoted favorable reception of the *Ship of Fools*, especially in England, is the work's heavy use of proverbs. The inclusion of so many, like the inclusion of woodcuts, made the work accessible and relevant to an extremely wide audience interested in practical ethical wisdom. This use of proverbs has been discussed by many scholars.[46] However, the importance of proverbs in Barclay's version is all the more noteworthy since the Latin version he relied on had omitted many of Brant's vernacular sayings.[47] Barclay not only greatly expanded this emphasis but also added many specifically English proverbs, so that David Anderson contends that "there is hardly a page, and certainly not a chapter" in which they do not appear.[48] However, as Anderson notes, this interest in proverbs reflects not only the work's popular and vernacular emphases but also a humanistic interest likewise apparent in the *Adagia* of Erasmus.[49] In his use of proverbs as in other ways, Barclay seems to have been a largely unacknowledged innovator, for according to the literary historian A. M. Kinghorn, Barclay was

> the first man to have current sayings printed in English, though his proverbs were an integral part of his principal works and were not intended to be isolated. Few passages in *The Ship* are

> without these worldly wise utterances. By the time of Elizabeth's accession, they had become a desirable attribute of polished literary style and every educated man was writing them.[50]

However, just as the *Ship of Fools* combined native, classical, and humanist interests in proverbs, so it also blended material from other genres, particularly vernacular and classical satire and medieval sermons. Brant's allusions to Horace, Persius, and Juvenal cascade down his margins, and humanists applauded the resemblances.[51] The Latin version added further classical allusions, and R. M. Alden has called Barclay's adaptation "the starting point of classical influence in English satire."[52] Other scholars, such as John Peter, have seen the work as "a *mélange* of Satire and Complaint," and both the unified temperament and apparent plotlessness of the *Ship of Fools* can be seen as appropriate to satire.[53] Gillis has examined Brant's debts both to the urbane satire of Horace and to the fiercer satire of Juvenal, whose influence she sees as decisive,[54] although other scholars have suggested that Brant and Barclay were both merely dressing medieval ideas in classical garb.[55] These scholars stress the impact of native satirical traditions,[56] the dance of death,[57] *memento mori* themes and attacks on vanity,[58] and the heritage of vernacular writings on fools.[59]

Yet the most important native source stressed by scholars consists of popular, homegrown sermons, which may have affected both the form and content of the *Ship of Fools*, especially since both the *Ship* and the sermons emphasized many classical *exempla*.[60] Scholars such as Klaus Manger,[61] David Anderson,[62] John Peter,[63] and especially G. R. Owst[64] have stressed the crucial influence of sermons on the creation, imagery, and reception of the *Ship of Fools*. Anderson notes that Barclay, as a priest, would have known this tradition well, and he cites Owst and others to show that the poem's style—which mixes the sacred with the profane and the learned with the quaint and homely—is completely typical of native preaching.[65] Although such similarities led John Berdan to claim that Barclay was "not a poet but a preacher" whose "works are no more satires than is a sermon,"[66] and although Koebling argued that "in spite of [Barclay's] learning, his point of view is entirely medieval,"[67] the distinction probably did not trouble Barclay's early readers. Indeed, the Latin version Barclay used specifically stressed the poem's links to the Roman satirical tradition, and Brant himself has been aptly described as a literary classicist.[68] The classical and humanistic features of the *Ship of Fools* have been well documented, especially by Ulrich Gaier, who detailed Brant's classical rhetorical patterns.[69] Both Brant and Barclay drew on many sources, including the classics, the Bible, the Church Fathers, and vernacular writings.[70]

Although it is possible to assert that the views of Brant are basically medieval, and although it is common to claim that Barclay is even more medieval than Brant, such careful demarcations can seem rather pedantic.[71] If the *Ship of Fools* reflects what we call a medieval mind-set, it was nonetheless hugely popular in what we call the Renaissance. If Barclay's work was influenced, directly or indirectly, by such medieval writings as those of Lydgate, Langland, Nigel de Longchamps, and various others who remain anonymous,[72] the *Ship of Fools*, probably through his printed editions, affected such Renaissance writings as those of John Awdelay, Robert Armin, Robert Burton, Robert Copland, Thomas Dekker, Robert Greene, Ben Jonson, Thomas Nashe, Samuel Rowlands, Reginald Scot, Richard Tarlton, Aston Cockayne, and numerous anonymous writers.[73] The complicated connections between Brant, Barclay, Erasmus, More, and Skelton are too tangled to discuss here,[74] and in general the impact of the *Ship of Fools* on Renaissance writers requires much fuller exploration. John Marston and John Milton allude to it, for instance, and Dekker, Gabriel Harvey, and Nashe seem to have been particularly affected.

Perhaps it is worth citing a few of these later references (some previously identified, others not) in order to give some sense of the wake the *Ship of Fools* left behind. Thus Gabriel Harvey, attacking Thomas Nashe in *Pierces Supererer-*

ogation (1593), at one point refers to "imbark[ing] the hardy foole in the famous Ship of Fools of wisemen," at another to "officiously recommend[ing him] to the Ship of Fooles, and the Galeasse of knaves," and at yet another to "a famous arrogant conceited foole, the very transcendent foole of the Ship."[75] Meanwhile, Nashe himself in *Pierce Pennilesse* mocks sycophants, flatterers, and favorites by writing: "Thus do weedes grow vp whiles no man regards them, and the Ship of Fooles is arriued in the Hauen of Felicitie, whilst the scoutes of Enuie contemne the attempts of any such small Barkes."[76] Similarly, in *Summers Last Will and Testament*, Nashe makes Will Summer remark that "If I had thought the ship of fooles would haue stayde to take in fresh water at the Ile of dogges, I would haue furnisht it with a whole kennell of collections to the purpose."[77] Moreover, in his Preface to Sidney's *Astrophil and Stella*, Nashe himself vows to "keepe pace with Grauesend barge, and care not if I haue water enough to lande my ship of fooles with the Tearme (the tyde I shoulde say)."[78] Evidently the *Ship of Fools* had made an indelible mark on the mind of one of the greatest Elizabethan satirists, and it seems likely that many more echoes will turn up in other writers as we acquire the means to search them more systematically.[79]

At least two allusions to the *Ship of Fools* appear, for instance, in the works of Thomas Dekker. Thus, in *Patient Grissill* (co-written with Henry Chettle and William Haughton) Babulo, a clown, exclaims, "There's a ship of fooles ready to houst sayl; they stay but for a good winde and your company: ha, ha, ha, I wonder, (if all fooles were banisht) where thou wouldst take shipping."[80] Meanwhile, Dekker's *Guls Horn-Booke* suggests that "if any person aforesaid, longing to make a voyage in the ship of Fooles, would venture all the wit that his mother left him, to liue in the contry of *Guls*, *cockneyes*, and *coxcombs*; to the intent that, haunting *theaters*, he may sit there, like a popiniay, onely to learne play-speeches, which afterward may furnish *ye* necessity of his bare knowledge, to maintaine table talke, . . . [etc]," he should know the *Horne-Booke* by heart.[81] Likewise, in his play *King John and Matilda* (probably dating from the late 1620's or early 1630's), Robert Davenport has a character declare that "your Barge stands ready/ To bear ye all aboard the ship of Fools," while Richard Brathwaite (1588–1673), in a poem entitled "The Critical Ape" (published in 1658), offers a similarly explicit allusion.[82] Similarly, Michael Drayton knew not only Barclay's pastoral poems but also the 1570 edition of the *Ship of Fools* in which they were printed,[83] while Milton casually alludes to "that famous ship of fools" in his sixth "Prolusion."[84] However, among the most interesting of all the later references are the extremely numerous echoes of the phrase and concept throughout John Marston's play *The Fawn*, especially in its final two acts.[85] His play, probably dating from 1604, simply takes the whole idea for granted, and Marston seems to assume that both his theatrical audience and his readers would have no difficulty making sense of his terminology. Like the quote from Milton, Marston's references to the *Ship of Fools* assume that it was still famous nearly a century or more after its initial publication.

Of course, whether the various allusions just mentioned refer to the German original, the Latin translation, the French translations, or the two English translations is usually difficult to determine, but in any case they all show that the *Ship of Fools* was definitely part of the early modern consciousness. The fact that it could be mentioned so casually by so many different authors suggests how well the work was known (at least by reputation), and the continuing allusions to it must also have stimulated a continuing interest in it. Each time the *Ship of Fools* was mentioned by an English writer addressing an English audience, some curiosity about Barclay must have been stirred. Such allusions, therefore, probably both reflected and stimulated an interest in the *Ship of Fools*.

For these reasons and others, Barclay's edition probably had an influence we have hardly begun to assess. Zeydel has suggested that Brant's *Ship of Fools* made such an impact because he gave a new form to native satirical impulses, and elsewhere he has suggested that Brant and Barclay helped turn literature away from allegory and toward drama, the essay, and the novel.[86] Are these assertions true, and in particular are they true of Barclay? Once again, we know too little to say very much, although Herford sees Barclay as an influence on the development of the Theophrastan character in England,[87] and various scholars have seen his work as an influence on, if eventually superseded by, the rise of Elizabethan drama.[88] Certainly the casual references by such dramatists as Nashe, Marston, and Dekker which have been quoted above suggest as much.

Given its demonstrable popularity in the Renaissance, why is Barclay's book so little read today? The simplest explanation, and the one championed by C. S. Lewis in his influential history of sixteenth-century literature, is that its poetry has no poetic merit. Lewis, who is at his caustic best when evaluating Barclay's writing, says (for instance) that with Barclay "we touch rock bottom"; that "his poetry has no intrinsic value"; that the *Ship of Fools* is worse than Barclay's other works "in so far as it is longer"; that as poetry it "is nothing"; and (most amusingly) that it is "hair-raising" to be told that Watson's version is even worse.[89] Other writers have anticipated or agreed with Lewis,[90] although even hostile witnesses such as these sometimes see merit in Barclay's writing.[91] Indeed, some readers have even expressed genuine enthusiasm. James McPeek, for example, has praised Barclay's tone of "impressive sincerity,"[92] and Aurelius Pompen has said that Barclay is "in many respects superior to Skelton."[93] David Anderson claims that Barclay uses his ship imagery more clearly than does Brant,[94] while Berdan credits Barclay with introducing "a satiric force, a downright plainness, and a concreteness" lacking in much earlier English writing.[95] Moreover, Berdan also praises Barclay for his "boisterous, rough, colloquial vigor,"[96] while A. M. Kinghorn calls the *Ship of Fools* an "entertaining work" whose "short chapters and constantly changing personages make for great variety of interest."[97] According to Kinghorn, Barclay's version "is more imaginative and colourful than Brant's," is "packed with allusions and spiced with wit," and therefore "deserves independent consideration as a fascinating example of the poetry of complaint."[98] Finally, Jamieson has claimed that Barclay's work is, "both in style and vocabulary, a most valuable and remarkable monument of the English language,"[99] and he asserts: "In the long barren tract between Chaucer and Spenser, the Ship of Fools [sic] stands all but alone as a popular poem, and the continuance of this popularity for a century and more is no doubt to be attributed as much to the use of the language of the "coming time" as to the popularity of the subject."[100]

How, then, do we account for Barclay's undeniable present status as a largely unread writer? Although Zeydel asserted that "Barclay writes a pure, natural English, which attempts to bridge the gap between the language of scholarship and the vernacular,"[101] and although Jamieson contends that such diction makes Barclay "infinitely more easy to read" than either Chaucer or Spenser,[102] it must be admitted that most modern readers would not find Barclay's *Ship of Fools* smooth sailing, if in fact they could find it at all. Not only is the work's language old-fashioned by today's standards, but the work exists in no easily accessible modern edition. Moreover, even the extant editions present serious problems (see Appendix, below).

Partly for these reasons, paradoxically, Barclay's book—which was once respected as a highly significant text—has now become as marginal as the fools it sought to excoriate. At one time Barclay spoke for (or at least sought to enunciate) the most important values of his period. Now, though, his voice is barely audible. Until we can hear it more clearly, we cannot begin to appreciate the importance of his text, either for his era itself or for our own attempts to understand that era. Although the general significance of his book is clear enough from its highly unusual publication and reception, its *specific* significances remain to be explored. Any temptation to assess them now in detail should probably be resisted: we simply do not (and cannot) know enough to speak at present with any assurance. Yet we do have many needed tools at hand: we have all the questions raised by the German *Narrenschiff* and the scholarship it has provoked; we have all the insights and problems offered by recent historical study and literary theory; and we have all the lessons and mistakes learned from working with similar texts to guide us.

In salvaging Barclay's *Ship of Fools*, then, we have the opportunity to explore with open eyes a work of undeniable historical significance—a work that has not been frequently visited and therefore a text that may yield (and provoke) more insights than we might at first expect. On the one hand Barclay's *Ship of Fools* may seem extraordinarily remote from our own interests and concerns, but in fact it is a work that resonates with many problems that preoccupy us today. These include the intersections of literature and history; the links between visual and verbal media; and the nexus of high and low, popular and elite, tradition and innovation. The *Ship of Fools* not only invites but demands to be read from the pespective of "intertextuality," and it poses many questions relevant to recent debates about "subversion" and "containment," the "radical" and the "reactionary," the "political" and the "asethetic." Clearly it speaks to our contemporary interest in the ways cultures define themselves by defining "others," but at the same time it speaks to more traditional debates about the transition from "medieval" to "Renaissance" or about the links between classical and Christian values—or about the rise, fall, and reciprocal influence of literary genres. Barclay's *Ship of Fools* remains a huge but largely unexamined artifact of a fascinating civilization; exploring it will inevitably reveal much, both about his society and also our own.

Barclay, of course, did not and could not speak for an entire culture, but his voice was obviously important. It resonated: when Barclay spoke, many of his contemporaries and their descendants listened and agreed. To open our ears to Barclay, then, is to become attuned to important currents in the culture of his and later times. To listen as Barclay tries to define, segregate, and punish his fools is to overhear an important cultural debate. Whatever its worth as poetry, as a historical source the *Ship of Fools* is of the very greatest value; the points of cultural conflict it touches are both encyclopedic and revealing. Barclay's efforts to impose rational order on his seemingly senseless times have much to tell us about the ways life was conceived, defined, and experienced as England took its first hesitating steps into the early modern era.[103]

APPENDIX

T. H. Jamieson's text of Barclay's *Ship of Fools* is usually cited as the standard edition, and for its day it was indeed a genuine accomplishment; however, it was first printed in 1874 and, in spite of a reprint issued by AMS Press, will not be found in most libraries. Its old-spelling text has the advantage of being in Roman type (rather than black letter), but Jamieson's decision to preserve Barclay's original punctuation, although a wise scholarly choice, makes for a text that, on the one hand, is sometimes nearly incomprehensible to a modern non-specialist reader and, on the other, remains subject to the ways of nineteenth-century editors. In addition, although Jamieson appends a useful glossary, he offers no explanatory notes, and he prints the more detailed and attractive woodcuts from the *Narrenschiff* rather than the cruder ones provided by Pynson for Barclay's version. Perhaps the most serious defect of his edition, however, is that he deletes all the many citations of classical and Christian writers that filled the margins of Barclay's text, nor does he include Locher's Latin version, which was originally interleaved with Barclay's translation. Of course, Jamieson was not preparing a definitive edition; he was simply trying the make the poem more accessible to nineteenth-century bibliophiles. Today, however, his edition leaves much to be desired both as a scholarly text and as a text for readers.

The closest thing to a genuine modern scholarly text is the

fine dissertation completed by David Anderson in 1974. Unfortunately, however, Anderson's edition is even less accessible than Jamieson's. Although the text is only lightly annotated, Anderson does provide a useful index and a full and sensible introduction, but he omits the woodcuts, nearly all the Latin of the original edition, and (most unfortunately) the classical and biblical marginalia. All these latter features are of course present in the reprint of the 1509 edition published by Da Capo Press in 1970,[104] but that edition lacks any critical or scholarly apparatus, is not widely available, and presents real problems of legibility for most modern readers. It is the most reliable text, but it is hardly the most readable.

What seems needed, then, is an edition that can make Barclay's poem accessible, both physically and linguistically, to the widest range of readers (especially students). A text modernized in typeface, punctuation, spelling, and syntax might not recapture for Barclay his old popularity, but it would at least allow him to speak anew to new generations. At the same time, such a text could easily include the missing marginalia, and it could be fully indexed, glossed, annotated, and introduced. It might even include appendices similar to those found in the important *Index Emblematicus,* now being issued by the University of Toronto Press—appendices which provide thorough guides to the links between the texts and illustrations of Renaissance emblem books.

A brief example may illustrate the kind of edition I have in mind. The following stanza, for instance, is the first from Barclay's chapter dealing with "falshode / gyle / and disceyte / & suche as folowe them" (fol. ccvvii^{v}).

> The vayne & disceytfull craft of alkemy
> The corruptynge of wyne and other marchandyse
> Techyth and sheweth vnto vs openly
> What gyle and falshode men nowe do exercyse
> All occupyers almost / suche gyle dyuyse
> In euery chaffar / for no fydelyte
> Is in this londe / but gyle and subtylte

The stanza helps explicate the accompanying woodcut (see fig. 8), and I have suggested elsewhere that both the cut and the ensuing text may have had some indirect influence on Ben Jonson's famous play *The Alchemist.*[105] The fact that this potential link seems not to have been noticed before is no doubt due to the fact that Barclay is today so little read (because so difficult to read). In the facsimile reprint, for instance, the black-letter typeface only exacerbates the problems caused by spelling, diction, and punctuation, which all pose difficulties for modern readers. Although this stanza is not nearly as difficult for modern readers as are many others, even it becomes clearer when modernized, as follows:

> The vain and deceitful craft of alchemy,/ the corrupting of wine and other merchandise,/ teacheth and showeth unto us openly/ what guile and falsehood men do now exercise./ All occupiers◦ almost such guile devise/ in every chaffar;◦ for no fidelity/ is in this land, but guile and subtlety.[106]

◦ occupiers: those who practice specific occupations
◦ chaffar: chaffer = trade or kind of business

A modernized edition might help us better appreciate Barclay's impact on his age and might make his work easier to read and thus easier to study. It might also give us a new sense of Barclay's merits as a poet (such as they are); after all, previously his verse has been hard to judge in part because it has been hard to read. In any case, such an edition, now in preparation, would provide easy access to an important poem and to a significant historical document—a sunken, ignored shipwreck stuffed with information about a crucial era in English social, intellectual, and literary history.

NOTES

[1] See Edwin Zeydel, *Sebastian Brant* (New York: Twayne, 1967), pp. 97, 102.

[2] Edwin Zeydel, Introduction, in his translation of Brant's *Ship of Fools* (New York: Dover, 1944), p. 24; hereafter cited as Zeydel, "Introduction."

[3] Ibid., p. 24.

[4] Alexander Barclay, *The Ship of Fools*, ed. T. H. Jamieson (Edinburgh: W. Patterson, 1874), p. ix.

[5] Zeydel, "Introduction," pp. 24–31.

[6] John Walter Van Cleve, *Sebastian Brant's* The Ship of Fools *in Critical Perspective, 1800–1991* (Columbia, S.C.: Camden House, 1993), p. 85; F. Schultz, Introduction to Sebastian Brant, *Das Narrenschiff* (1494; facs. rpt. Strassburg, 1913), as quoted in Zeydel, "Introduction," p. 24.

[7] Yuichi Midzunoe, "Alexander Barclay and the *Ship of Fools*," *Renaissance Bulletin*, 12 (1985), 9–12.

[8] Gary Waller, *English Poetry of the Sixteenth Century* (London: Longman, 1986), pp. 27, 38.

[9] C. H. Herford, *Studies in the Literary Relations of England and Germany in the Sixteenth Century* (Cambridge: Cambridge Univ. Press, 1886), p. 368.

[10] See, for example, David Rollin Anderson, "A Critical Edition of Alexander Barclay's *Ship of Fools* (1509)," Ph.D. diss. (Case Western Reserve Univ., 1974), p. 41; G. R. Owst, *Literature and Pulpit in Medieval England* (New York: Barnes and Noble, 1961), p. 55; Aurelius Pompen, *The English Versions of the Ship of Fools* (1925; rpt. New York: Octagon Books, 1967), pp. 4–6; and Zeydel, "Introduction," p. 32.

[11] R. M. Alden, *The Rise of Formal Satire in England Under Classical Influence* (Philadelphia: Univ. of Pennsylvania, 1899), pp. 15, 18.

[12] See Arthur Koebling, "Barclay and Skelton: Early German Influences in English Literature," in *The Cambridge History of English Literature*, ed. A. W. Ward and A. R. Waller (Cambridge: Cambridge Univ. Press, 1907–33), III, 63–70, esp. 69. See also Zeydel, "Introduction," p. 104.

[13] See Koebling, "Barclay and Skelton," p. 69; Herford, *Studies*, p. 372.

[14] David Carlson, "Alexander Barclay," in *Sixteenth Century British Nondramatic Writers*, 1st ser., ed. David A. Richardson, Dictionary of Literary Biography, 132 (Detroit: Gale, 1993), pp. 36–47, esp. 36 and 46.

[15] James A. S. McPeek, *The Black Book of Knaves and Unthrifts in Shakespeare and Other Renaissance Authors*, Univ. of Connecticut Publications Ser. (Storrs: Univ. of Connecticut, 1969), p. 48; Zeydel, "Introduction," p. 39.

[16] Anderson, "A Critical Edition," p. 66.

[17] See Zeydel, "Introduction," p. 17.

[18] See Owst, *Literature and Pulpit*, p. 232; Anderson, "A Critical Edition," p. 94; Pompen, *The English Versions*, p. 308.

[19] See Zeydel, *Sebastian Brant*, p. 95; Anderson, "A Critical Edition," p. 69.

[20] Herford, *Studies*, p. 327.

[21] See Barclay, *Ship of Fools*, ed. Jamieson, p. xvi; and also Helmut Rosenfeld, "Brants *Narrenschiff* und seine Stellung in der Publizistik und zur Gesellschaft," in *Beiträge zur Geschichte des Buches und seiner Funktion in der Gesellschaft: Festschrift für Hans Widmann zum 65. Geburtstag am 28. März 1973*, ed. Alfred Swierk (Stuttgart: Hiersmann, 1974), as cited by Van Cleve, *Sebastian Brant's* Ship of Fools, p. 76.

[22] Barclay, *Ship of Fools*, ed. Jamieson, p. xvi.

[23] See Patricia Gillis' "Introduction" to Sebastian Brant, *The Ship of Fools*, trans. William Gillis (London: Folio Society, 1971), p. xi.

[24] Thomas Cramer, "Der bildniss jch hab har gemacht:—Noch einmal: Zu Text und Bild im *Narrenschiff*," *Beiträge zur Geschichte der deutschen Sprache und Literature* (Tübingen) 111, No. 2 (1989), 314–15, esp. 332; as cited in Van Cleve, *Sebastian Brant's* Ship of Fools, p. 82.

[25] Henry Charles Lea, "The Eve of the Reformation," in *Cambridge Modern History*, ed. A. W. Ward, G. W. Prothero, and Stanley Leathes (London: Macmillan: 1903–11), I, 683, as quoted by Gillis, "Introduction," pp. xviii–xix.

[26] Hans-Georg Kemper, *Deutsche Lyrik der frühen Neuzeit*, I: *Epochen- und Gattungsprobleme* (Tübingen: Niemeyer, 1987); as cited in Van Cleve, *Sebastian Brant's* Ship of Fools, p. 81.

[27] Anton Zijderveld, *Reality in a Looking-Glass: Rationality Through an Analysis of Traditional Folly* (London: Routledge and Kegan Paul, 1982), p. 80.

[28] Van Cleve, *Sebastian Brant's* Ship of Fools, p. 53, citing Bernard Ohse, "Die Teufelliteratur zwischen Brant und Luther: Ein Beitrag zur näheren Bestimmung der Abkunft and des gestigen Ortes der Teufelsbücher, besonders im Hinblick auf ihre Ansichten über das Böse" (Ph.D. diss., Free University of Berlin, 1961), p. 55.

[29] Van Cleve, *Sebastian Brant's* Ship of Fools, p. 60, citing Barbara Könneker, *Wesen und Wandlung der Narrenidee im Zeitalter des Humanismus: Brant—Murner—Erasmus* (Wiesbaden: Steiner, 1966), p. 132.

[30] Van Cleve, *Sebastian Brant's* Ship of Fools, p. 17, citing Friedrich Zaracke's Introduction to his edition of [*Das*] *Narrenschiff* (Leipzig: Wigand, 1854), p. lxxvi.

[31] Zijderveld, *Reality in a Looking Glass*, p. 82.

[32] Hellmut Rosenfeld, "Die Entwicklung der Ständesatire im Mittelalter," *Zeitschrift für deutsche Philologie*, 71, No. 2 (1952), 196–207, esp. 206–07; as cited by Van Cleve, *Sebastian Brant's* Ship of Fools, p. 51.

[33] Van Cleve, *Sebastian Brant's* Ship of Fools, pp. 73–74, citing Robert Weimann, *Realismus in der Renaissance: Aneignung der Welt in der erzählenden Prosa* (Berlin and Wimer: Aufbau, 1977), esp. pp. 67–68.

[34] Kenneth J. Northcott, "The Fool in Early New High German Literature: Some Observations," in *Essays in German Literature—I*, ed. F. Norman (London: Institute of Germanic Studies at the University of London, 1965), p. 42; as cited in Van Cleve, *Sebastian Brant's* Ship of Fools, p. 52. In paraphrasing the Marxist view, Van Cleve (p. 50) cites Joachim G. Boeckh *et al.*, *Geschichte der deutschen Literatur von 1480 bis 1600*, Geschichte der deutschen Literatur von den Anfängen bis zur Gegenwart, 4 (Berlin: Volk und Wissen, 1960), p. 216.

[35] Van Cleve, *Sebastian Brant's* Ship of Fools, p. 78, citing Helmut Birkhan, "Zum Erfolg des *Narrenschiffes*: Sebastian Brant und die Tradition," in *La representation de l'antiquite au moyen age: Actes du Colloque des 26, 27, et 28 Mars 1981*, ed. Danielle Buschinger and André Crepin (Vienna: Halosar, 1982). See also Anderson, "A Critical Edition," p. ii.

[36] Owst, *Literature and Pulpit*, p. 232.

[37] See Barbara Swain, *Fools and Folly During the Middle Ages and the Renaissance* (New York: Columbia Univ. Press, 1932), pp. 117, 129.

[38] Zijderveld, *Reality in a Looking Glass*, p. 80.

[39] Gillis, "Introduction," p. xx.

[40] Ibid., p. xxi; and Swain, *Fools and Folly*, p. 127.

[41] Anderson, "A Critical Edition," p. 69.

[42] Barbara Tiemann, "Sebastian Brant und das frühe Emblem in Frankreich," *Deutsche Vierteljahrsschrift für Literaturwissenschaft und Gesitesgeschichte*, 47 (1973), 598–644; as cited by Van Cleve, *Sebastian Brant's* Ship of Fools, p. 76; Herford, *Studies*, p. 369; Swain, *Fools and Folly*, pp. 118–20; and Holger Homann, "Emblematisches in Sebastian Brants *Narrenschiff*?" *Modern Language Notes*, 81 (1966), 463–75, as cited by Van Cleve, *Sebastian Brant's* Ship of Fools, p. 70.

[43] Anderson, "A Critical Edition," p. 69.

[44] Ibid., pp. 69–70.

[45] See ibid., p. 77.

[46] These include, for example, Hans Eberth (see Van Cleve, *Sebastian Brant's* Ship of Fools, p. 41); Anderson, "A Critical Edition," pp. 93, 98; and Van Cleve himself, p. 62.

[47] Pompen, *The English Versions*, p. 311; Anderson, "A Critical Edition," p. 95.

[48] See Anderson, "A Critical Edition," p. 95; Koebling, "Barclay and Skelton," p. 68; and also John M. Berdan, *Early Tudor Poetry, 1485–1547* (New York: Macmillan, 1920), p. 251.

[49] Anderson, "A Critical Edition," pp. 96–97. For Erasmus' *Adagia*, see Desiderius Erasmus, *Adages*, trans. Margaret Mann and R. A. B. Minors, Collected Works of Erasmus, 30–34 (Toronto: Univ. of Toronto Press, 1982–92), 4 vols.

[50] A. M. Kinghorn, *The Chorus of History: Literary-Historical Relations in Renaissance Britain* (New York: Barnes and Noble, 1971), p. 172.

[51] Zeydel, *Sebastian Brant*, p. 82; Van Cleve, *Sebastian Brant's* Ship of Fools, pp. 60–61; Anderson, "A Critical Edition," p. 82; Gillis, "Introduction," pp. xv–xvi.

[52] Zeydel, *Sebastian Brant*, p. 92; Alden, *The Rise of Formal Satire*, p. 17.

[53] John Peter, *Complaint and Satire in Early English Literature* (Oxford: Clarendon Press, 1956), pp. 10–11. See also Gillis, "Introduction," p. xvi, and Anderson, "A Critical Edition," p. 84.

[54] Gillis, "Introduction," pp. xvi–xviii.

[55] See Anderson, "A Critical Edition," pp. 84–85.

[56] Ibid., pp. 84–85, and Van Cleve, *Sebastian Brant's* Ship of Fools, p. 72.

[57] Rainer Gruenter, "Die 'Narrheit' in Sebastian Brants *Narrenschiff*," *Neophilologus*, 43 (1959), 207–21, esp. 210–13; cited by Van Cleve, *Sebastian Brant's* Ship of Fools, p. 56.

[58] Karin Singer, "Vanitas und Memento Mori im *Narrenschiff* des Sebastian Brant (Motive und Metaphern)," Ph.D. diss. (University of Würzburg, 1967), pp. 212–13, as cited by Van Cleve, *Sebastian Brant's* Ship of Fools, p. 71.

[59] Anderson, "A Critical Edition," p. 20.

[60] Ibid., pp. 85–87.

[61] Klaus Manger, *Das "Narrenschiff": Entstehung, Wirkung und Deutung* (Darmstadt: Wissenschaftliche Buchgesellschaft, 1983), p. 123, as cited in Van Cleve, *Sebastian Brant's* Ship of Fools, p. 80.

[62] Anderson, "A Critical Edition," pp. 39, 91.

[63] Peter, *Complaint and Satire*, p. 61.

[64] Owst, *Literature and Pulpit*, pp. 55n, 69.

[65] Anderson, "A Critical Edition," pp. 100, 114.

[66] Berdan, *Early Tudor Poetry*, p. 251.

[67] Koebling, "Barclay and Skelton," p. 69.

[68] See Gillis, "Introduction," pp. xiv–xvi; see also Berdan, *Early Tudor Poetry*, p. 248.

[69] See Ulrich Gaier, "Sebastian Brant's *Narrenschiff* and the Humanists," *PMLA*, 83 (1968), 266–70; cited by Van Cleve, *Sebastian Brant's* Ship of Fools, pp. 60–63; Anderson, "A Critical Edition," pp. 102–06; Zeydel, *Sebastian Brant*, p. 79.

[70] See Van Cleve, *Sebastian Brant's* Ship of Fools, p. 85; Anderson, "A Critical Edition," p. 87; Barclay, *Ship of Fools*, ed. Jamieson, pp. xiii–xiv.

[71] See Van Cleve, *Sebastian Brant's* Ship of Fools, pp. 73–74; Pompen, *The English Versions*, p. 307; Anderson, "A Critical Edition," p. 11; Berdan, *Early Tudor Poetry*, p. 254.

[72] See Herford, *Studies*, p. 327; Anderson, "A Critical Edition," pp. 24–25, 27–28, 40; Zeydel, "Introduction," p. 9; Zijderveld, *Reality in a Looking Glass*, p. 79.

[73] See Herford, *Studies*, pp. 331, 357, 364–65, 370–75; Zeydel "Introduction," pp. 39–42; Alden, *The Rise of Formal Satire*, p. 22; and Koelbing, "Barclay and Skelton," pp. 62, 68. For a more recent assessment, see Lawrence Manley, *Literature and Culture in Early Modern England* (Cambridge: Cambridge Univ. Press, 1995), pp. 79–88. I am grateful to Professor Manley for responding to a query over the internet.

[74] See, for instance, Herford, *Studies*, p. 324; Anderson, "A Critical Edition," pp. ii, 10, 31, 34–39, 55–65; Alden, *The Rise of Formal Satire*, p. 22; Koebling, "Barclay and Skelton," pp. 69–70; Carlson, "Alexander Barclay," p. 39; Zeydel, "Introduction," pp. 40, 43–45; and Zeydel, *Sebastian Brant*, p. 105.

[75] Gabriel Harvey, *Pierces Supererogation* (London, 1593), pp. 70, 140, 150; for the corresponding passages in the nineteenth-century edition, see *The Works of Gabriel Harvey*, ed. Alexander B. Grosart (London: Huth Library, 1884), II, 125, 221, 235. I owe these references to Professor William Barker, who very kindly responded to a query over the internet.

[76] Thomas Nashe, *The Works*, ed. Ronald B. McKerrow (London: Sidgwick and Jackson, 1910), I, 175.

[77] See ibid., III, 257–58.

[78] See ibid., III, 332.

[79] The fact that most of the current standard editions for Renaissance writers (especially the less prominent ones) lack subject indexes makes searching difficult. As more and more texts become available in electronic versions, more and more allusions to the *Ship of Fools* will probably be found.

[80] Thomas Dekker, *The Non-Dramatic Works*, ed. Alexander B. Grosart (London: Huth Library, 1884–86), V, 157.

[81] Dekker, *Non-Dramatic Works*, II, 204. For another allusion by Dekker to the idea of a ship of fools, see his pamphlet *The Seuen Deadly Sinnes of London* (1606), in *Non-Dramatic Works*, II, 61. I owe this latter reference to Professor John Leonard, who helpfully responded to an internet query.

[82] Robert Davenport, *King John and Matilda: A Critical Edition*, ed. Joyce O. Davis (New York: Garland, 1980), pp. xii and 78 (III.v.27–28); Richard Brathwait, *The Honest Ghost, or a Voice from the Vault* (London, 1658), p. 9. I owe these references to the kind help of Eric Smith, a reference librarian at the Duke University Library.

[83] See Michael Drayton, *The Works*, ed. J. William Hebel (Oxford: Blackwell, 1931–41), II, 518.

[84] "Prolusion VI," trans. David Masson, in John Milton, *The Works*, ed. F. A. Patterson *et al.* (New York: Columbia Univ. Press, 1931–40), XII, 204–05.

[85] I am grateful to Professor Frank Whigham for calling this aspect of the play to my attention. According to Morse S. Allen, "The idea of Barclay's 1509 translation of Brandt's [sic] *Narrenschiff* furnished a kind of rallying point for Marston's satire in this play—the collection of all kinds of folly for exile. The Ship of Fools is mentioned by name no less than eleven times in the play, while V,i is devoted to a court in which classes of foolish lovers are successively sentenced to the ship. Marston borrowed little or nothing from this book except the name" (*The Satire of John Marston* [1920; rpt. New York: Haskell House, 1971], pp. 152–53).

If anything, Allen's counting of references to the *Ship* is a bit too conservative; see, for instance, the following passages in the edition of *The Fawn*, ed. Gerald A. Smith (Lincoln: Univ. of Nebraska Press, 1965): I.ii.31; III.i.133; IV.i.81, 84, 171, 175, 178, 191, 203–06, 217–18, 512–14; V.i.45; 48, 231, 269, 289–90, 359, 377–78, 413.

[86] Zeydel, *Sebastian Brant*, p. 103; Zeydel, "Introduction," p. 39; see also Koebling, "Barclay and Skelton," p. 69.

[87] Herford, *Studies*, pp. 325, 378.

[88] Ibid., pp. 327, 370–72, 377; Zeydel, "Introduction," pp. 42–43.

[89] C. S. Lewis, *English Literature in the Sixteenth Century Excluding Drama* (London: Oxford Univ. Press, 1954), pp. 129–31.

[90] See Berdan, *Early Tudor Poetry*, p. 253; Koebling, "Barclay and Skelton," p. 67; Waller, *English Poetry of the Sixteenth Century*, pp. 27, 38; Zeydel, "Introduction," p. 28.

[91] See Berdan, *Early Tudor Poetry*, p. 254; Koebling, "Barclay and Skelton," pp. 68–69; Zeydel, "Introduction," p. 29.

[92] McPeek, *The Black Book of Knaves*, p. 48.

[93] Pompen, *The English Versions*, p. 3.

[94] Anderson, "A Critical Edition," p. 49.

[95] Berdan, *Early Tudor Poetry*, p. 254.

[96] Ibid., p. 254.

[97] Kinghorn, *The Chorus of History*, p. 167.

[98] Ibid., p. 166.

[99] Barclay, *Ship of Fools*, ed. Jamieson, p. xx.

[100] Ibid., p. xxi.

[101] Zeydel, "Introduction," p. 29.

[102] Barclay, *Ship of Fools*, ed. Jamieson, p. xx.

[103] For additional helpful suggestions in preparing this article, I wish to thank Professors Michelle A. Laughran (Univ. of Connecticut) and A. B. Coldiron (Univ. of Virginia), who graciously responded to a query over the internet.

[104] Alexander Barclay, *The Ship of Fools*, The English Experience, 229 (Amsterdam: Da Capo Press, 1970).

[105] See Robert C. Evans, "Jonson and the Emblematic Tradition: Ralegh, Brant, the Poems, *The Alchemist* and *Volpone*," in *Emblem, Iconography, and Drama*, ed. Clifford Davidson, Luis R. Gámez, and John H. Stroupe (Kalamazoo: Medieval Institute Publications, 1995), pp. 108–32, esp. 112–24.

[106] Stanzas would be printed as prose not only to conserve space but to promote ease of reading; for a similar format, see Guido Waldman's translation of Ariosto's *Orlando Furioso* (London: Oxford Univ. Press, 1974).

Following the model provided by the *Index Emblematicus*, the accompanying woodcut might be described as follows:

> Standing before a ◦furnace or ◦oven containing a spouted ◦flask and a large ◦pot or ◦pan, a ◦fool grabs or stirs the pot with a ◦ladle or ◦tool of some sort. Another man, in more dignified dress, stands behind him and also holds a spouted flask, and several other pots and spouted flasks are on the floor beneath the furnace. Another fool is kneeling before a ◦barrell, apparently ◦tampering with the ◦wine it contains.

Staging Folly in the Early Sixteenth Century: Heywood, Lindsay, and Others

Peter Happé

I

The first half of the sixteenth century was of particular importance for the development in England of the idea of folly and the stage role of the fool. There is not much evidence of the fool as such on stage before Skelton, the main manifestations being some foolish characteristics of the vices in *Mankind* and the role of Stultitia in *The Castle of Perseverance*.[1] Certainly the activities of fools, natural and artificial, can be documented in abundance in real life at court and in the houses of the nobility throughout the Middle Ages. For example Enid Welsford instances Golet, the fool of William of Normandy in 1047, and Sandra Billington notices Hitard, jester to Edmund Ironside.[2] That we do not find the fool on the English stage very much may partly be occasioned by the paucity of morality plays before 1500, but I should like to suggest that there are some reasons why he became more popular as a stage figure in the first half of the sixteenth century. These may be considered partly conceptual in that an evolving idea of the fool epitomized in Erasmus' *Praise of Folly*, written in 1509 (for Sir Thomas More) and published in 1511, comes into consideration; and there is also, I suggest, a deepening awareness of the theatricality of the fool. Perhaps the latter is rather hard to separate from the former and should be considered concomitant and complementary, but one of the chief aspects of my argument in this paper concerns the way in which dramatists discovered they could make use of the fool on stage because of the advantages he offered.[3]

Though the court fool no doubt evoked laughter and was indispensable for entertainment, the common medieval idea was that fools were evil because they knew no God—an idea promoted by the opening verse of Psalm 52 (Vulgate numbering).[4] Further, there was the view that all people, men and women, were fools because they were sinners. The most important aspect of this may have been human irrationality in a world that Aquinas held was substantially and divinely rational.[5] One poetic manifestation of this was Stephen Brant's *Narrenschiff* (1494), translated by Alexander Barclay as *The Ship of Fools* (1509).[6] The poem probably influenced Skelton in *The Bowge of Court* where he took the interesting satirical step of directing ridicule at the court that had a prominent role in his poetry. However, Skelton made one important change in allowing the narrator to include himself as an example of folly:[7] an aspect that anticipates *Magnyfycence* in a number of ways.

The possibility that fools were evil was never forgotten, but to it was added, chiefly through the influence of Erasmus who in turn derived from St. Paul, the concept that the fool was also holy and that his folly was wiser than wisdom. It is perhaps this combination of paradoxes which proved so fruitful for the dramatists considered in the present essay. Erasmus achieved his paradoxical view of the fool by his personification of Folly and by making her both a fool herself and a wise, if mischievous exposer of and commentator upon other fools. Because Erasmus chose the quasi-dramatic device of a monologue, he put the reader (like a member of an audience) into the position of being able to agree with what she says and also of being able to object to her commentary. Walter Kaiser points out that Erasmus specifically distances himself from Folly's pronouncements, perhaps because it would be dangerous to be too explicit, yet this may be an effective part of the fiction.[8] Erasmus' two-edged presentation may well have been one of the most important aspects of his influential book for dramatists, though one may note that the conventions of the *sottie* which were rather similar were presumably becoming established some time before he wrote his book.[9] The play of irony which has Folly declare that she is indispensable to human happiness is both a continuation of the medieval condemnation of folly and a humanist emphasis on the dictum that folly can teach us all.[10] Barbara Swain, tracing the impact of Erasmus, has characterized it as a shift towards "unreasoning love."[11]

Against this intellectual background we may consider the preoccupations of dramatists interested in making the most of situations on stage in a combination of entertainment and instruction. While, as I have suggested elsewhere, Skelton in *Magnyfycence* may have owed something to the conventions of the *sottie*,[12] his English inheritance, being less concerned with fools, offered instead a moral world encapsulated and symbolized in allegory. For Skelton, I suspect that the possible, perhaps inevitable breakdown of this structured universe was deeply unwelcome and had to be resisted, but for the two principal writers whose work is to be considered here the change was a fact of life that had to be accepted and indeed to be managed according to their different beliefs: Heywood took a humanist Catholic position, and Lindsay was nearer to Protestantism. Both Heywood and Lindsay were not only closely involved in a royal court but survived in such milieu for a long time, in contrast to Skelton. Perhaps even more strikingly than Skelton's, their work shows a marked adaptation of the French plays which used fools.

Theatrically the fool offered a number of advantages. He could be inside the action of the play as a character, even as a person professionally engaged within the world of the play earning his living by entertainment. He could be an embodiment, in an allegorical manner, of the folly of other characters in the play who might be either human or personified abstractions. His unlimited ubiquity made it possible for him to mix with other fools, with human characters, and with abstractions. Though I do not wish in any way to impugn the allegorical mode of earlier morality plays, in an evolving dramatic context, facing a different age and using new styles of theatrical presentation, it would not be surprising if dramatists saw folly as a useful device for diversifying their dramatic method. The fool could be detached from the activities of others with a potential for commentary or for a variety in dramatic mode. Though none of the dramatists considered here took over the notion entirely, Erasmus' presentation of the universality of folly, explicit also in the *sotties*, remains an underlying possibility undermining the activities of all characters.[13]

Since part of the excitement of drama may well be the way the writer plays upon the response of the audience, the possibility that folly offers differing, even conflicting feelings in play simultaneously makes the use of this figure particularly attractive. Such ambiguity may well be deeply satisfying to an audience. The dramatization of folly has both a moral dimension (as outlined above) and an emotional component. The latter turns upon the gaiety of fools, with all the performance paraphernalia of jokes, costume, hats, properties, gesture, movement (including dancing), in contrast with the fatalism that is inherent in the inevitability that all are fools, and that all human activity is foolishness. Since the culpability of folly never quite disappears, it could be easily revived, especially for polemical or even quasi-tragic purposes. Indeed the effectiveness of folly on stage can be seen particularly in the satire of all ranks of society, a dramatic objective which, though inherited from medieval eschatology, remained a key feature of Renaissance plays. Perhaps the shift towards a bourgeoisie in the theater was an invitation for folly, especially as characterization according to social position continued to be an attractive mode.[14] The plots involving folly demonstrate that the structural importance of the desire for fantasy and also for justice could be effective material for the stage. This is not to say that such expectations need be entirely fulfilled. In the case of justice, for example, the possibility that it might not be achieved is a deeply intriguing structural effect.[15]

II

In turning to the plays of John Heywood and the extent to which he sought to dramatize fools and folly, we may bear in mind some features of his inheritance, the complexity of the problem of a dramatic realization, and the nature of some other dramatizations immediately after him.[16] One of the objectives is to place observable aspects in terms of the period in which Heywood was writing and also of the context of the Court drama.

Heywood wrote his plays in several different styles. *Witty and Witless*, which contains his most extensive and most theoretical treatment of the subject and which will claim much attention in what follows, may have been the earliest of his extant plays: it is certainly written in a dramatic form which is different from the rest, closer to the *Colloquies* of Erasmus than are his other plays, though this is not to say that there are not distinct performance characteristics in it, and there is also supporting evidence that Heywood did have performance in mind. Whatever the influences upon Heywood's work, it may well be suggested that he modified his sources extensively, within the limitations of the theatrical resources and conventions available to him in the 1520's and 1530's, in a direction that points to Shakespeare's embodiment of folly into his comic universe; but such a hindsight should not be allowed to obscure the perception of Heywood's achievement for what it is. The investigation should also show to some extent his application of folly towards religious and political objectives.

The title of *Witty and Witless* was given to the manuscript of this play in the eighteenth century. It is close to the central subject of debate, whether the witty or the witless has more pleasure and more pain, but it does polarize a disputation that actually is played out by three voices and that is concerned with an argument on two levels, pleasure and/or pain. In other words, the debate is found to be more three or even four dimensional than the title may suggest. As such it depends upon a number of characteristics of folly. Interestingly, Heywood uses the word "sot" frequently to indicate the natural fool, while the more evil artificial, calculating counterpart hardly comes into the discussion except in a rather limited way in the second half of the play. James, a somewhat impertinent participant, takes the view that the fool is in a more desirable state because his social position is protected in that it is not necessary for him to labor to earn his bread. James adds that emotionally the *sot* is safer because he cannot suffer the pains of mind that the witty person experiences. Brushing aside John's claims that the fool is a victim of harsh treatment, including the whip, and that being emotionally unstable he gets very upset if he loses such a trifling item as a Walsingham whistle, James caps the first part of his argument by showing that the *sot* has one sure expectation, the pleasure of salvation which must outweigh everything else (l. 335). By contrast, he claims that the witty man must suffer doubt about his salvation, and he may indeed never attain it. Thus, according to James, there are two temporal reasons and one spiritual reason why the fool's state is preferable, and John, conceding the case, brings the first part of the argument to an end. J. B. Altman characterizes this first part as the thesis and the second part as the antithesis,[17] but we should add that there are two broad arguments—that fools are wiser than the wise, and that human reason makes a positive contribution to salvation—which represent conflicting interpretations of folly (see below).

Jerome, whose name may be an indication that Heywood was conducting this argument with the interests of Catholic orthodoxy in mind, enters the argument in the second half of the play with the intention of vindicating the non-fool, but significantly he changes the name and consequently the nature of the latter from Witty to Wise (so that really the play might have been dubbed *Witless, Witty, and Wise*): "Wysdome governth wytt alwey vertu to use,/ And all kynds of vyce alway to refewse" (ll. 423–24). This change means that the *sot* is now seen as the opposite of the wise man, and by implication the characteristic in the *sot* of being culpably foolish in that he is not being wise is now brought into question. Jerome is interested in showing John the mistakes he had made in conceding to James. This shift in objective on Heywood's part has perhaps not been sufficiently recognized as an indication that underlying the pleasure of this witty exchange of views there is a serious moral and religious purpose and one which is close to the public arguments of the late 1520's when Catholic theology was being defended against Lutheran incursions. The play may be constructed as a game of wit, as Altman suggests, but the purpose is far from being superficial enjoyment. The dynamic or indeed dramatic structure of the play points unmistakably to this by the introduction of the issue of the fool's salvation in the first half of the argument and by the subsequent direction of the whole of the second half towards the question of the relationship between good deeds in this life and the experience of the world to come. Another important sign of the direction of the argument is that James, the advocate of the superiority of the fool's situation, is now withdrawn from the dispute.

A good deal depends now upon the place of reason in the argument, an issue that links up with a number of other plays of the period, especially Henry Medwall's *Nature* and John Redford's *Wit and Science*. The personification of Reason later interested Heywood himself when he came to write his lost play on the Government of Reason for Cranmer (c.1545–48).[18] One should bear in mind also that Reason was held to be one of the chief strengths of Thomist theology, which saw it as an important support for faith.[19] Jerome introduces the idea that it is better to use human reason than to be a millhorse. This idea is close to Reason's speech in the later play:

And the diffrens between man the kommaunder
And beasts being by man kommaunded
Is only Reason in man, the disserner
Of good and ill, the good in man elekted
By me, and th'ill in man by mee rejekted.[20]

John at length concedes the point, whereupon Jerome demonstrates that the fool, who does not use his reason, is indistinguishable from an animal in this respect. The point may well be an echo from Erasmus: "A natural fool differs from a brute beast only in bodily appearance."[21] There are also precedents for the idea of the importance of activity of the mind in the pursuit of wisdom: "Do you think one is human if he's neither wise nor wants to be wise?" And wisdom is "understanding that a man is not happy without the goods of the mind."[22]

So much for this life: there follows a consideration of the next in which Jerome, following a reference to words of Christ and to an exposition by St. Augustine (ll. 559–64), makes clear that the rewards of heaven are commensurate with the good works done on earth: "Syns God to the most faythfull wurker gyvythe most" (l. 637). The acquisition of merit here depends upon the exercise of the will as well as the use of reason, and the deeds involved are closely related to the good works that are central to the argument between Catholic and Protestant at this time.[23]

The argument of Jerome is supported at several places by cross reference to "Sot Somer," Will Somer, the real life fool of Henry VIII, who apparently came to Court in about 1525 and survived to the reign of Mary Tudor. His "presence" at the play—and by implication "in" it—is first established early: "Not evyn Master Somer, the Kyngs gracys foole/ But tastythe some tyme some nyps of new schoole" (ll. 43–44). For some reason not discernible in the text, Heywood chooses to mock Somer persistently and to equate him with the notional empty-headed *sot*, virtually a beast. Since the one stage direction in the manuscript envisages the possibility that the King might be present at a performance, it may well be that there was also an expectation that Somer would accompany him. However, the presence of the King alone would sharpen the point of Heywood's teasing. Somer is presented as being the equivalent of the millhorse, and Jerome brings the argument to an end by saying that it is much better to share the wisdom of Solomon, based upon reason, than the ignorance of Somer: "In for sakynge that I woolde now rather be/ Sage Saloman then sot Somer, I assewre ye" (ll. 659–60). This neatly reverses James' earlier (but now shown to be erroneous) assertion: "Better be sott Somer then sage Salamon" (l. 440).

Thus the treatment of folly here depends upon two key features of fool literature: the idea that fools are innocent, and as such they are embodiments of divine grace and protected by it, but also the belief that they are ignorant and that this ignorance may be a form of sin and potentially damnable. The general tone of Heywood's play, like most of his others, is essentially reasonable and not confrontational even though he does present conflicting arguments in vigorous language. Nevertheless, he is interested in making a substantial contribution to a political argument, especially since the King, not long before declared *Fidei Defensor*, might be present in the audience. It does appear as though Heywood's plays were aimed at performance at Court, by boys' companies, but equally they might have been staged before influential aristocratic audiences associated with it. Certainly the payments to Heywood in connection with other dramatic performances, not, unfortunately, for any of the extant plays, are very much in the Court environment.[24] Heywood's language in *Witty and Witless* is also a significant feature since it is rich in pithy proverbial sayings, as are his other plays, not to mention the *Dialogue of Proverbs*.

Witty and Witless may well have been influenced by the French tradition of fool plays, especially the farces and the *sotties*. This is not easy to prove. Nevertheless, the play was written at a time when such entertainment was popular in France, and there is no doubt that *Johan Johan* was a direct translation from a French farce. A precedent for reference to French conventions in *sotties* may lie in Skelton's *Magnyfycence,* which was probably produced in or near the Court in about 1518 and which was printed in 1529. This latter date is particularly opportune to the initiation of Heywood's plays and to the subsequent publication of some of them in 1533 and 1534. The presence of the idea of the fool and his nature and role in society, together with the use of the term *sot,* provide circumstantial evidence that there was a link between *Witty and Witless* and some French plays. More specifically, it has long been suggested that Heywood may have made use of *Le Dialogue du Fou et du Sage,* which was printed between 1516 and 1527 and again before 1532.[25] The exchange between Sage and Fou turns upon the former's decision to turn wise, rejecting the folly of his former life. But Fou alleges that Sage's criteria depend upon success in this world, and he exploits this weakness by trying to show that all Sage will be gaining cannot compare with the security Fou now has in having nothing and valuing nothing in this world, not even a good reputation. Fou's arguments depend upon scripture in several places, and he alleges that Sage is in fact tempted by avarice.[26]

> Davoir argent ce nest que dueil
> Et tout soucy de le garder.[27]
>
> (Having money is only grief,
> and looking after it is trouble.)
>
> Iamais ioye tu nauras.[28]
>
> (Thou wilt never have happiness.)
>
> Mais un pauvre homme qui na rien
> Iamais il ne craint le deschet.[29]
>
> (But a poor man who owns nothing
> will never fear its loss.)

Fou actually wins the debate, and Sage accepts his winning argument: "Tel est fou qui cuyde estre sage" ("He who thinks himself wise is a fool").[30] This interpretation of folly which stresses its ubiquity and also suggests that the Fool is not too stupid *sub specie aeternitatis* leads to the position of Erasmus in his *Praise of Folly*, but Heywood's presentation of folly in *Witty and Witless* places more emphasis upon the role of reason, and he gives more weight to positive religious virtues which may be identified as Catholic.

In Heywood's other plays there is, I suggest, a continuing use of the notion of folly, though there is no comparable, sustained discussion of fools as such in any of them. Perhaps the strongest aspect of the consciousness of folly lies in the idea that folly rebounds upon itself in making the perpetrator look foolish because the results or implications of his actions show up his weaknesses. While a moral implication may be involved here, folly itself also consists of being inconsistent, impotent, or ridiculous. The latter quality is an important dramatic effect, and it may be the result of a complex tricking procedure or it may merely leave the audience to perceive the enjoyable effects of folly.

Both these aspects appear in the role of Neither loving nor loved in *A Play of Love*. He is undoubtedly the crudest of the four characters in actions and language, as his physical examination of Lover not loved shows (ll. 1022–31). His role is also the biggest part and one which prompts a number of developments in the action. For these reasons, perhaps, he is called the Vice in one stage direction. There is a possible link between the Vice and the stage fool inasmuch as both rely heavily upon a repertory of stage devices and a vigorous stage presence to manipulate the attention of the audience; however the Vice, when fully developed later in the sixteenth century, is always evil, whereas it is one of the purposes of the present essay to show that the fool is not always so.

Neither loving nor loved concentrates much of his actual ridicule upon the Lover loved, who is in some respects his "opposite," though Heywood plays a dazzling game of similarities and dissimilarities in the interacting of the four characters in this play as well as in the physical movements on stage. His verbal mockery appears in calling him a "Woodcock" as often as possible as part of his attempt to show his own superiority since he claims that by not loving and not being loved he avoids the pains of love in "contynuall quyetyd rest" (l. 376). In fact the term 'Woodcock' is tantamount to 'fool' in that the Vice says to Lover loved "Wyll ye gyve me leave to call ye fole anone,/ When your selfe perceyveth that I have proved you one?" (ll. 333–34). His position in the complex of experiences of love by all the characters is finally presented as inadequate because of what it misses, and it recalls the role of the fool in *Witty and Witless*: safety is foolishly perceived to be found in not taking part and in not taking risks while love merely brings physical and mental stress (ll. 1188–96). But this exposure of folly in Neither loving nor loved is not the perception of a moral evil as such: it is much more a delicate exposition of a failure of love, and here Heywood cleverly links sexual with divine love.

The Vice's ridicule turns more active towards the end of the play when it is apparent that he cannot win the argument with his opposite by words. He disappears suddenly only to return grotesquely clad, with squibs exploding and an enormous copintank hat on his head, proclaiming fire (l. 1297 *s.d.*).[31] His explanation that he has seen a young woman answering to the description of Lover loved's beloved in a house afire sends his victim rushing off in manifest panic. He appears to have made his point about the pains of love sensationally, but when Lover loved returns he meets the argument by saying that he responded to Neither loving nor loved's lie and not to truth. The two participants agree that the argument is a draw. However, Neither loving nor loved's position is then refuted by the conclusion of the play because the latter turns the subject of love to a more philosophical and indeed religious mode by asserting the power of divine love (ll. 1543–77). The implication is that the Vice's active attempt to expose folly in others is itself foolish.

Such a conclusion is anticipated in the other weighty aspect of his part, his long narrative on the theme *moccum moccabitur* (ll. 399–690). As this is performed as a solo (ll.

407–08), the audience is challenged either to take what is said at face value or to see it ironically, and of course the latter is the case. The Vice claims that although he apparently indulges in a passionate affair he outwits his lover by not really loving her, and he leaves her high and dry (ll. 592–607). However, he relates that after an absence of (only) half a day "[m]y harte mysgave me" (l. 609); he returns out of pity only to find her in bed with another. She tells him that she has got her own back, that she saw through his insincerity, and that he, the mocker, has been mocked. Heywood introduces the language of folly specifically by having him admit that this looks as though he were made a fool: "thyncke my selfe or any man elles a foole/ In mockes or wyles to set women to scoole" (ll. 663–64). But he claims that since he did not love her in the first place he has avoided jealousy. Bringing back the argument to his victim and sparring partner, Lover loved, he concludes that "Reason shall so temper his opinion/ That he shall see it [love] not worth an onyon" (ll. 683–84). But presumably the audience cannot agree with his self-satisfaction and now reads his protestations otherwise. Though the Vice may still have in him the power to continue to ridicule the Lover loved, he has in fact given the impression that he is not fireproof, and in this way he is a victim of his own folly. Whatever the mocker achieves, he cannot escape mockery, and thus his position is not unlike that of Folly in the *Praise of Folly*.

In the remaining four plays by Heywood the treatment of folly is less direct, but as we shall see the use of impertinence, verbal games, and some actions which show up the foolishness of various characters suggests that the exploitation of folly for stage purposes was never very far from his thoughts and that the place of folly in his plays was a technique which could be made to serve differing objectives. Such dramatic strategies may well have been rooted in Heywood's role as a provider of Court entertainment. It should be remembered too that folly on stage could be active or passive. On the one hand the fool may be the voice of truth showing up the foolishness of all others, and on the other the fool himself is part of a world of folly from which he cannot escape. Indeed it is worth recalling the comment of the late Jean-Claude Aubailly on the *sottie*: "La folie n'est pas le sujet mais un mode d'expression et de communication."[32] Ultimately the *sottie* may have shown a world of confusion and disintegration, but with Heywood there is at least a sense that the presence of folly and its techniques may be part of a more positive and perhaps specifically religious conception of the universe or at least a conception that needed to be defended pragmatically at a time of disturbing change.

Religious matters are addressed in *The Pardoner and the Friar* in that the bulk of the play consists of the attempts of these two ecclesiastical characters to ply their trade, ostensibly for the good of the listeners but actually for purposes of heresy and avarice. As Ian Maxwell has shown, the play probably owes something to *La farce d'un Pardonneur, d'un Triacleur et d'une Taverniere*.[33] In both plays the itinerant quacks compete for attention, changing from an apparently benign beginning to a curse at the end. But if Heywood was influenced by this particular farce, he certainly made significant changes, especially in substituting the Friar for the Triacleur, thus bringing into question the dishonesty in religious persons which was a concern of Erasmus and his followers. For the Pardoner he followed Chaucer, from whom he derived some of the same relics, though when he departed from his source he added outrageous ones of his own which may have been inspired by those in the farce. For example Heywood's play has "Of All Helowes the blessyd jaw bone" (l. 154) and the farce "le groing Du pourceau monsieur sainct Anthoine" ("the snout of M. St. Anthony's pig").[34] Surely these fantasies are manifestations of folly.

The most significant innovation onstage is probably having the two chief characters speak simultaneously. It is a highly entertaining process, but it also has the effect also of making them look ridiculous and making what they say less credible. In short, this is one of the ways by which they are made to look like fools. To perform in this manner, of course, requires considerable skill on the part of the actors. The five passages of simultaneous speech gradually becoming more vehement build up tension between the two characters to such an extent that they fall to blows, at which point their credibility as men doing good disappears altogether.

But the purpose of the play is fully consistent with Erasmian critique of abuses in the Church in respect to the Pardoner. With regard to the other character in the play, Heywood may have been following More's lead in ridiculing the Friar as though he were a heretic, perhaps reflecting upon Luther's attack on indulgences since he takes upon him the power of freeing souls from guilt. The play contains some references to the language of folly and thus keeps up the sense that these men ultimately are ridiculous.[35] It is notable that they are both very unattractive characters (unlike some of the characters in *The Four PP*, which recalls *The Pardoner and the Friar* in some respects). If the Pardoner and the Friar are fools they are of the sinister kind, well able to manipulate language for their own selfish ends. It is a specially potent aspect of the paradox of folly that these two ecclesiastical characters should be so far from grace. Instead of the positive pursuit of true religion which we see Heywood consistently seeking in most of the other plays, this drama tends instead to be a negative exposure of superstition. It is not surprising that after their fight with one another they turn to violence against the Parson and the Constable, Church and State. The Pardoner makes the Constable's blood run down, while the Friar "dothe the upper hande wyn" (l. 637) against the Parson. Having thus joined forces, they leave with a threat: "Than adew, to the devyll, tyll we come again!" (l. 640). It is a note that anticipates the later Vice, who is usually evil.

Heywood's *Four PP* may be likened to *A Play of Love* in that it shows four characters of differing stance who compete with one another on virtually equal terms and who seek to settle their differences by argument. These two plays, together with *Witty and Witless*, may recall the *sottie* where all the characters are *sots* together and where the action consists of the resolution of a difficulty, with the characters being a group of similar but differentiated members. Once again the structure of the play does not depend upon a plot centered upon action and events: the true action is the development of attitudes towards these characters as they reveal themselves and rival one another, and in the approach to a resolution of conflict, though this is not necessarily a closure. Though the handling of folly is implied rather than specifically emphasized, there are a number of references which suggest that Heywood was using it as part of his technique. For example, near the beginning of *The Four PP* the initial argument between the Palmer and the Pardoner shows the latter has folly in its most derogatory sense in mind: "Nowe is your owne confessyon lyckely/ To make your selfe a fole quyckely" (ll. 89–90). Similarly, on his first entry the Poticary bluntly tells these two characters that he will "by the leve of thys company/ Prove ye false knaves bothe or we goo" (ll. 158–59). Later the Pardoner, resenting the interruption of the Poticary, condemns him as a "daw" (l. 359).[36] The dialogue itself is rich in a number of devices which recall the language of folly, some of it in the French tradition. Among the most prominent is the use of leashes where the ingenuity of elaborating on the same sound draws attention to the sentiments which are in themselves part of the mode of folly. In the case of the elaboration upon "pyncase" the purpose is bawdy (ll. 243–52), as the language of folly so often is, and the game with words ending in "-ettes" points up a joke about female vanity (ll. 257–62).

Possibly Heywood again had a French farce in mind in making two of the characters present themselves as tricksters.[37] There is more than a hint that these fools are the dishonest sort who will indulge in anything to make money and to talk themselves out of trouble. However, Heywood's moral control, which is consistent with the

Catholic humanist doctrine, is actually interested in moving such questionable activities towards love and tolerance. Nevertheless he allows extensive demonstration of shady practices with regard to the Pardoner's relics, some of which derive from Chaucer, and the Poticary's remedies. Part of the entertainment in this fooling lies in the fantastic excuses which are given for it, as, for example, when the Poticary claims that he is useful as a means of getting to heaven since hardly anyone gets there without his assistance. His impertinence is complemented by his logic.

The questionable moral tone is also sustained by the Pedler's suggestion that they should establish their superiority by means of a competition in lying. It is a fantastic idea quite appropriate to fools in the French tradition. However, the introduction of the competition in lying is actually part of Heywood's strategy to bring out more serious elements. In the first place there is an argument between the Poticary, the Pardoner, and the Palmer about what is necessary for salvation. The Pedler turns this aside on the grounds that he is not competent to give judgment on such a profound matter: "Ye know it is no whyt my sleyght/ To be a judge in maters of weyght" (ll. 384–85). Instead he is the one to make the suggestion that their contest should be about lying. This device actually makes it more interesting when the competition is over and the serious matter of tolerance and love is raised in its place at the end. The pursuit of such a trivial, foolish, but very entertaining false trail is part of the strategy of the playwright: the foolish way brings the audience around to a truth in the working out of another version of the wisdom/folly paradox. This indirect strategy may be considered alongside the fact that Heywood avoids in all the extant plays the traditional morality structure of fall/life-in-sin/rise: in this respect his plays are a significant shift towards the French *sotties* and farce.

Since there is now no doubt that *Johan Johan* is a translation of *La Farce du Pasté*, Heywood's interest in and use of the French presentation of folly has been made clear.[38]

The translation is a close one which suggests that Heywood felt that for most of the time the original spoke for him, and yet we shall note several departures which help to make more precise his sense of folly. The original shows how the Man (not named) is befooled sexually by his Wife and the Priest. All the characters are conventional, and a good deal of the dialogue also fits established patterns. Thus Heywood's plot begins with Johan's account of his own misery over Tib's sexual adventures, his own misfortunes, and his wish to be revenged by beating her. His manhood is in question both through her infidelity and through his need to assert himself. But as soon as she appears his aggression evaporates:

> *Tyb:* Why, whom wylt thou beate, I say, thou knave?
>
> *Johan:* Who, I, Tyb? None so God me save. (ll. 111–12)

He quickly becomes only a foolishly impotent husband. The main action of the play shows Tib and the priest, Sir John, enjoying a pie and by implication one another, while Johan, sitting by the fire and aware of all that is going on, has neither pie nor Tib. At the same time he is forced to mend a hole in her pail and chafe the wax for it. The scene is arranged so that there is an increasing tempo of frustration and humiliation on Johan's part while the other two become more and more explicit in their language and presumably in their actions. Finally in both versions the husband explodes into violence and beats the other two, but Heywood's change in the ending suggests that even then Johan has great doubts about whether he has done anything effective to stop Tib's "catterwauling":

> For, by God, I fere me
> That they be gon together, he and she,
> Unto his chamber, and perhappys she wyll
> Spyte of my hart, tary there styll,
> And peradventure there he and she
> Wyll make me cokold, evyn to anger me:
> And then had I a pyg in the wors panyer. (ll. 669–75)

Johan's reduction to foolishness is complete.

This change in the translation is accompanied by a number of others such as the adopting of English saints and proverbs for the French ones (as in the "panyer," above), but in the matter of folly Heywood's substitution of English phraseology is significant: the "martyrdom" of the French becomes "By cokkes soule, I am a very wodcok" (l. 488).[39] He also intensifies the repetition of key phrases such as "chafing the wax," and he develops very considerably the sexual language which is present but less explicit in the French. In both versions the Priest tells three tales about the conception of children. Heywood chooses, however, to alter the content of all three apparently to show more directly that this priest had intervened personally to bring about conception. In the first there is the phrase "Yf she had not had *the help of me*" (l. 548); in the second "She was delyvered of a chylde *as moche as I*" (l. 566); and in the third "*I knewe* a nother woman eke ywys" (l. 576). Once again Heywood is pursuing the wrongdoing of the clergy, and although Johan is made a fool, both Tib and Sir John are pointedly victims of folly.

A consideration of some possible sources or influences upon *The Play of the Wether* may help to reveal the underlying reference to folly. In this case the *Dialogues* of Lucian of Samosata, which probably reached Heywood through the Latin translations from Greek by Erasmus and More from 1511 onwards, may have suggested such details as Jupiter's attention to a range of conflicting petitions from earth, his use of a volunteering, nimble doorkeeper named Mercury, and the problem of access as well as reference to the weather as a source of anxiety.[40] However, two French farces which turn upon the interrogation of petitioners by a *sot* acting on behalf of superior authority have been identified by Maxwell: *La Reformeresse* and *La Mere de ville*.[41] Possibly in some way the Lucian material informs the *sotties*, but Merry Report and his handling of affairs may have been given a particular aura because it worked by suggesting French farce. The language of folly is suggested by many details of Merry Report's dialogue, including his bawdy exploitation of the Gentlewoman and the Laundress, his punning on the words of the petitioners, his mockery of Jupiter who is making a new moons behind the curtain, and his tendency to let his mockery run in leashes such as we see in *Witty and Witless, A Play of Love,* and *The Four PP*. He generally offers a merciless exposure of all whom he meets, and he particularly ridicules Court behavior so that no one comes out with honor. All may be regarded as selfish fools, unable to see any view except their own. The attempt to suggest that all ranks of society are implicated in the folly is also a factor. Certainly the treatment of Jupiter by Lucian may have been an influence, but there is little doubt, bearing in mind Heywood's other use of French farce and *sottie*, that Merry Report is a vehicle by which the idea of ubiquitous human folly is conducted in *The Play of the Wether*.

But the idea of folly is detachable from the exponents of it within the plays, and so it arises that Heywood uses folly for the wider political purpose of commenting upon the stress in Court over conflicting opinions. In the end his plea for tolerance is the most he can do to assuage the bitterness of controversy surrounding the King's Divorce and presumably More's part in the controversy. Most interesting is the timing of the printing of the play by William Rastell, More's nephew by marriage as well as his printer, just at the point when More was most concerned to change the current of events against the Catholic interest and before the legislation setting up the new Protestant hegemony. Probably Heywood wanted to keep things as they were and wished the King not to accede to factional clamor now surrounding him. At this point, concerning Heywood's pursuit of the idea that the King should be encouraged to assert his authority, the interpretation of the political objectives of *The Play of the Wether* suggested here is closest to that recently proposed by Greg Walker.[42] However, Walker dates the composition of the play at around 1529, whereas here the assumption is that the *publication* of the play in 1533 was a political intervention designed to sustain the King's independence against conflicting factions. By 1533 the issues surrounding the Divorce were momentously poised, and More was much more vulnerable: no longer Chancellor, he doggedly and provokingly pursued his outspoken political and religious controversy against the rising Protestant interest. Characteristically Heywood's intervention is different in tone from More's controversial fury in such works *The Confutation of Tyndale* (1532–33) and *The Debellation of Salem and Bizance* (1533). He instead uses comedy, without bitterness or vituperation, with folly playing its part, but this does not mean that there was not an underlying serious purpose. Of course, many of the French plays, both farce and *sottie*, also in their turn had specific political circumstances in mind and sought to bring pressure on those in power.[43] The King was now using the threat of Protestant ideas as a means of achieving his own ends over the Divorce, and it is not surprising that he was showing some interest in Protestant writings such as Tyndale's *The Obedience of a Christian Man* of which he expressed approval.

III

The above comments upon Heywood's use of folly not only as a vehicle for an exploration of religious matters but also as an important element in stage technique may be supplemented by a consideration of the anonymous *Godly Queen Hester*, Nicholas Grimald's *Archipropheta*, and John Redford's *Wit and Science*.

The political context of *Godly Queen Hester* may well be the period just before the fall of Wolsey, as Walker has suggested, since the play is an attempt to encourage Henry VIII to take power into his own hands.[44] Assuerus, the king in the play, is threatened and deceived by Aman, and it is the business of the action to show how the latter's misdeeds develop and eventually how they are countered by Queen Hester. The folly element is concentrated upon

Hardydardy, who plays but a small part in two episodes. If the play really is dated 1529 he may be a very early example of the Vice convention, though he is not so named. His function is to prophesy Aman's wrongdoing and to moralize after the fall of Aman.

Like the Vice, he is heartless and an exponent of wordplay, but his role is not so large as most of the later examples: he does not appear until line 636 in a play of 1180 lines. Moreover, his identity seems to incline more to fool than Vice: there is no hint about costume to help us decide. Entering with a proverb, he declares his intention to become one of Aman's servants, but Aman is cautious and, seeing him rather in the role of fool, decides to keep him "for our solace/ And mirthe sumtime to ken" (ll. 683–84). The dialogue in which this occurs (ll. 656–94) is really an exchange about the relative merits of the fool and the wise person. Hardydardy attacks the wise for their inherent folly, while Aman takes a moral line:

> *Hardydardy:* And wyse men will say nought at al till al be gone and more.
> *Aman:* Fooles to Idlenes all wayes be preste.
> *H:* And wyse men use such busines it were better they were at rest.
> *A:* Fooles let the reformation of common wele.
> *H:* And wyse men be so full of imaginacion,
> They wot not how they deale.
> *A:* Whyse men wolde do ryght,
> And foles say nay. (ll. 665–72)

Hardydardy sees the role of the fool as the entertainment of wise men, but he suggests that wise men may behave foolishly:

> *H:* I wene by goddes grace one foole in a place,
> Doth well amonge wise men
> Ye must nedes laughe amonge and if a foole sing a songe.
> I holde you than a grote
> Some wise man muste be fayn sumtime to take the paine
> To do on a foles cote. (ll. 685–90)

The effect of Hardydardy's intervention is to point to moral evil, but at the same time the paradoxical ambiguity of the relationship between wisdom and folly does not promise well for Aman. Accordingly, as things later become more dangerous he refers Aman to the prophecy made by Ambition, Pride, and Adulation (ll. 801–08).

Hardydardy's final contribution after the condemnation of Aman is to show by recounting the story of Phalaris that he was killed by his own device—"the fyrste taster/ Of his owne invencion" (ll. 1047–48).[41] His final remark is perhaps nearer to the Vice than to the fool, though there is still the sense that his playing with words contains some foolish wit: "Therfore God sende all those, that will steale mens clothes,/ That once they may goe naked" (ll. 1055–56).

The role of the fool as Court entertainer is exploited by Nicholas Grimald in his Latin play *Archipropheta*.[46] Gelasimus keeps the door of Herod's palace and declares (p. 258) that he is "king of the fools" ("Sum rex morionis"). He is bibulous and shows a lecherous interest in a Syrian girl, and he comments on the foulness of the world ("Profecto hic mundus est res immundissima") and the vanity of women (pp. 280, 282). His antics include a joke about having fifteen fingers and putting the jewels of Herodias on his head. He is struck for speaking the truth (p. 314) and complains that everyone hits him, even children. He claims that he has been in hell where he saw the Devil having Pharisees and women for breakfast (p. 320). Thus the emphasis is primarily upon performance: his moral impact, though mischievous, is not profound, and he has no part in the last act's terrible event, the decollation of John the Baptist. However, one should not overlook the Protestant weighting of the play working by means of a criticism of the court of Herod. The play was dedicated to the eminent Protestant divine Richard Cox, and the presumed date of the manuscript near the end of Henry VIII's reign was a delicate moment for Protestant fortunes.

John Redford's *Wit and Science* survives in British Library Add. MS. 15233, which also contains some poems by Heywood and others associated with the St. Paul's choir school.[47] Redford apparently took little interest in religious controversy or doctrine, and instead adopted an allegorical mode intended to explicate various aspects of learning from a humanist viewpoint. As the allegory shows, the hero Wit, who is expected to marry Science by her father Reason and her mother Experience, falls into temptation by Idleness; here the presence and influence of folly are made apparent by means of Ingnorance, but, as in Skelton's *Magnyfycence* and in *Godly Queen Hester*, its role is limited to certain episodes. The allegorical mode follows the morality structure of falling into sin followed by restoration. Within this broad structure there is embedded a fool sequence that is designed to bring about Wit's self-recognition, which is necessary if he is to achieve his marriage. This episode is of considerable importance structurally, for it provides the means by which Wit is instructed. It is also probably intended as an example for the young scholars who probably performed the play originally under Redford's direction.

The fool sequence shows Wit under the power of Idleness, a situation in no way likely to prepare him for the battle with Tediousness. Having danced with Idleness, Wit falls asleep, whereupon she demonstrates her relationship with her son Ingnorance whom she tries to instruct. But she is so frustrated by him that several times she calls him fool, and it is apparent that he is wearing a fool's coat. Together they take the garment of Reason from Wit and replace it with the fool's coat. At the same time they blacken his face. Ingnorance, the fool, seeing the change, says, "He is I now" (l. 599). Idleness comments that Wit is "conjurd from Wyt unto a starke foole" (l. 614). When the transformation is completed there follows the self-recognition of Wit, who is ignorantly unaware of his appearance as a fool. When he meets Science she quickly and repeatedly makes clear that she wants nothing to do with such a fool. She comments very pointedly:

> I take ye for no naturall foole
> Browght up a mong the innocentes scoole

> But for a nawghty vycious foole
> Browht up wyth Idellnes in her scoole.
> Of all arrogant fooles thow art one. (ll. 806–11)

Though if this were a realistic drama she would now seem not to know what has happened, her remark has a different purpose, for it is essentially allegorical: Wit is responsible for his own folly, and so he will have to make amends for it.

Angrily Wit looks at himself in the glass of Reason. The audience's anticipation is fulfilled as he sees what he has become. We need not follow out the rest of the allegory except to say that Wit must be punished and given new apparel before he can progress further towards his ultimate goal. Differentiated from that of Heywood, Redford's use of folly is strictly subservient to the allegory, and it reflects the traditional split between ignorant and clever fools. In the case of Ingnorance this is altered to make him, as the natural fool, also lacking in virtue or spiritual insight, save perhaps that he does correctly perceive that Wit is temporarily a fool.

IV

Sir David Lindsay's *Ane Satire of the Thrie Estaitis* is a remarkable blend of several different characteristics from late medieval drama. While it cannot be shown to have been directly influenced by *Magnyfycence* or John Bale's *King Johan*, it shares with them a concern for the position of the king in relationship to political and moral abuses, and it is deeply involved in the religious controversy of the time in the circumstances of the Scottish Court. To this extent and beyond Lindsay's drama is within the genre of the sixteenth-century morality play, but there are clearly other elements as well. The account of the original performance at Linlithgow Palace in 1540 contains no explicit reference to folly or to a fool, but the expanded versions relating to performances in 1552 at Cupar and 1554 at the Greenside, Edinburgh, show some revealing elements of folly both in terms of the idea of folly and in the action of some fools. There is little doubt that Lindsay was aware of the French conventions, especially since he had spent several periods at the French Court on diplomatic duties in the 1530's, apparently before he wrote his play.[48] In the earlier version Lindsay was interested in drawing the attention of James V to the need for reform in the Church, even though he was much less radical in his approach than Bale in *King Johan*.[49] In its later form in a more difficult political climate, with the Catholic Mary of Guise as Regent interested in reconciling religious extremists, the play was performed in the open air, at which time it seems likely that its mode of production was influenced by the large scale moralities that had been presented in France from the late fourteenth century.[50] But from the point of view of the study of folly it will be noted that there are a number of fool episodes which are in one sense outside the main allegorical action and purpose of the drama, but which emphatically complement it. I do not propose to examine the main moral preoccupations of this long and complex play in detail here but rather to concentrate upon showing how Lindsay adapts the fool elements within his broader intentions. These elements do not take over the play as a whole, but they do adapt some aspects of the staging of folly in a pointed and effective manner. They demonstrate that it was possible to move in and out of a fool mode.

There are two concentrated fool episodes: the Fule in the Proclamation, and Foly in the sermon at the end of the play (ll. 4301–4647).[51] The Cupar Proclamation, which must have been written for the performance at that location in 1552, contains a farcical episode showing how the Fule woos the wife called Bessy by deceiving the Auld Man, her husband. Here the characterization is like that of the French farce (and different from a *sottie*) inasmuch as the Fule seems real in himself as a character in a human situation. He may show broader aspects of folly, but he operates within the limited world of this domestic comedy. His link with lechery may be significant thematically, especially as Rex Humanitas is shown in Part I giving way to Sensualitie. There is also the possibility that this wooing has folk play analogues, especially the lecherous activities of Tom Fool and Dame Jane in the Plough Monday play.[52] That he happens to be a fool gives a further twist to the farce, but he is not really distinctive in Lindsay's handling of the playlet or separated in type from the other characters: he shows little of the special language of an embodiment of folly. If Lindsay was influenced by French farce here, he nevertheless translated his ideas into a distinctive Scottish idiom in a parallel manner to Heywood's adaptation of French farce to an English setting. There is a good deal of Cupar coloring here and probably some local jokes.

More substantial as well as distinctive is the sermon of Foly. Though the sermon may be viewed as an almost separate episode, it can be seen as having a definite bearing upon what has preceded it, indeed virtually everything in the play refers back to some previous material, so that it is an emphatic summing up of some of Lindsay's main preoccupations. Part II of *The Thrie Estaitis* is an extended presentation of reform in the state, with special attention to the role of the religious in the nation who are presented as largely corrupt and unfaithful to their vows. Lindsay was close to Reformation doctrines, though his treatment of them within the play is interestingly veiled, perhaps because he was, like Heywood, a long-term survivor at Court.[53] Nevertheless there is no doubt about his condemnation of abuses by the Catholic clergy, the bishops, abbots, and parsons—the whole estate represented by Spiritualitie throughout the two parts of the play—both in terms of their sexual aberrations and in terms of their interest in wealth. With regard to the latter it should be remembered that a good deal of Reformation politics was about a redistribution of wealth, though not necessarily on egalitarian principles. The case for the new Church is made in the sermon of the Doctour preached from the pulpit (ll. 3473–3586). Again the approach is not doctrinally radical, but the spiritual failure of the Catholic hierarchy is brought into question. It is notable dramatically that the speaker is interrupted at various times by the Abbot and the Persoune; for example: "Cum doun, dastart, and gang sell draiff,/ I understand nocht quhat thow said" (ll. 3560–61). After the speech, however, justice is done to the aberrant clerics, and after the proclamation of the new Acts in the Parliament the group of vices, with the exception of the slippery Flatterie, is also brought to book.

The Foly episode changes the mood considerably. He begins with an outrageous tale about an encounter with a sow, a complaint that he wishes to bring to the notice of the King. This is followed by an even more bawdy account of his wife which recalls the earlier abuse by the Sowtar of his Wife. He sits down to give breakfast to his daughter, Glaiks (glossed as "a foolish, senseless creature" by Hamer), and Stult, his son. In all these things, what he says may be unpalatable, but he is not presented as evil. Indeed much of what he says has the mysterious strength of a suggestion of a generality of truth. On being summoned to the King, he tells the audience about his less innocent sexual response to a girl he sees amongst them. The speech here recalls the Fule's comment in the Proclamation (Proc., ll. 160–62, and cf. ll. 4438–39), and probably both involve the obscene use of a phallic device, no doubt with accompanying gestures. He notices the pulpit, and is told about the sermon preached by the "Bishop" (i.e., the Doctour), whereupon his most extensive response is set off. If, he claims, the Bishop has taken to preaching, it will do harm to the interests of the friars, but so far he is apparently thinking of Catholic bishops. However, he offers to preach to the three Estaitis as he has some merchandise, his hats, for them, "For I have heir gude chaifery/ Till any fuill that lists to by" (ll. 4488–89). This is an indication that his sermon is to present the foolish state of those to whom it is addressed, and so it proves. So far structurally much of what has been said reflects elements earlier in the play. This concentrated, highly packed mode continues with the contents of the sermon itself which take up the ground prepared in the preamble.

It seems likely that Lindsay modeled Foly's speech on the *Sermon Joyeux*[54] since it sets out as a subject or theme a general description of folly that is found in them—"*Stultorum numerus infinitum*" (l. 4502)—though we have here a commonplace that was generally available.[55] Moreover, Foly provides a genealogy, begins with a blessing, and ends with a prayer that is to be made for the fool Cacaphatie, who recently has died. In addressing the Estaitis he shows their foolishness: the merchants for putting all upon hopeless ventures; the old man for marrying a young bride; the Spirituality for depending on "gredines of warldlie pelf" (l. 4569); and Kings and other leaders, including the Pope, for fighting against one another (ll. 3593–3606). The subject matter here may not be entirely associated specifically with the Reformation, but there seems little doubt that what he says is consistent with the failings of the clergy noted so extensively in the play. He uses the phrase "Gang backwart throw the haill cuntrie" (l. 4536) which recalls the spectacular entry of the Estaits at the beginning of Part II: "*Heir sall the Thrie Estaitis cum fra the palyeoun, gangand backwart led be thair vyces*" (l. 2324 *s.d.*). The folly of old husbands with young brides refers retrospectively to the earlier Fule episode with the Auld Man and Bessy. Foly's condemnation of the folly of Princes is anticipated by the attack on the papal conflict with France (ll. 3593–94). Moreover, the tone of the remarks, bitter as they are, suggests that this fool is to be believed, even though he has shown himself to be folly itself in the crudeness of his preamble. This is enhanced by the prosodic difference noted by John J. McGavin, who points out that the (by implication) deliberately disordered verse of the first part of the sequence is succeeded by a more serious passage (ll. 4502–4647) that is "prosodically consistent, using couplets throughout."[56]

The distribution of Foly's hats, which he has carried on in a basket and hung on the pulpit while he preaches, is a pointed reminder of the *sotties* in which all the characters were sometimes dressed in fools' costumes to show that they were fools.[57] As the dialogue shows—interestingly Lindsay has Foly questioned by Diligence as he proceeds —the purpose of the preaching is to identify folly in all those characters whom he mentions: "Ye ar all fuillis, be Cokis passioun" (l. 4586; the use of a blasphemous oath keeps him from appearing morally unassailable). He is particularly hard on the "Spirituall fuillis" that, while administering great dioceses and abbeys, foolishly lose their own souls: "Uthers sauls to saife it settis them weill,/ Syne sell thair awin saullis to the Devil" (ll. 4571–72). But it should also be noted that while attacking the prelates Foly quotes "*Sapientia huius mundi stultitia est apud Deum*" (l. 4528), a Pauline commonplace equating the wisdom of the world with folly in God's eyes (see *1 Corinthians* 3.19). An ironic note is struck by Foly's allegation that it would be foolish to attack the prelacy for fear of being found heretical (ll. 4579–80).[58]

These two fool episodes are the most concentrated scenes showing the use of folly in the play. They are also highly entertaining because of the stage opportunity offered by them, especially for a skilled actor. In other parts of the play, however, both the language and actions of folly are sustained. Flatterie, as we have noted, acts as a moral evil in a morality structure in which vices do their worst. Here the disguises and the aliases make them into deceivers of the King. Flatterie apparently arrives dressed in particolored clothes, a form of motley, "Begaryit all with sindrie hewis" (l. 604). That he disguises these clothes later under the habit of a friar may on the one hand be villainous deception, but it is also dramatically significant because the audience may well recall that underneath all is folly.[59] And the evil intent may have been sustained by the possibility that the ship in which he arrived may have been a ship of fools like Brant's, which, as we have seen, was essentially a view of folly as evil and damned. Flatterie's role here may also be a clue to other onstage presences in which the possibility of revealing of evil beneath clothing is present, especially for the religious characters, as indeed proves to be the case.

Folly is also emphasized by many occasions when individual characters are called fools. Usually these are points of identification of evil rather than a means of showing the kind of wise folly that Foly himself communicates in his sermon. Instead, many characters show themselves up as contaminated by self-destructive foolishness. For example Spiritualitie insists "I am na fuill" (l. 3391) when he is showing that his evil ways succeed, and the Abbot, having sent his sons to the schools of Paris, says "I traist in God that thay salbe na fuillis" (l. 3436). In fact, the folly demonstrated here has its climax when the prelates are despoiled of their garments, and possibly they are dressed as fools underneath, as the Merchant's observes: "Now men may se ye ar bot verie fuillis" (l. 3756). However, the general state of folly is developed further by Spiritualitie's immediate rejoinder: "We say the Kings war greiter fuillis nor we,/ That us promovit to sa great dignitie" (ll. 3757–58). And the Abbot adds: "Thair is ane thowsand in the kirk but doubt,/ Sic fuillis as we gif thay war weill socht out" (ll. 3759–60).

Earlier in the play the Pauper is called a fool by Diligence for hoping that the law will help redress his wrongs against the Church (l. 2015). Shortly afterward Pauper is engaged in a foolish dispute with the Pardoner over whether the pardon for a thousand years is worth the expenditure of a groat (ll. 2227–2300). While no direct mention of folly is made here, there nevertheless is a strong sense of making a fool in the episode.

Thus it is clear that Lindsay points up the abuses he wishes to underline by means of an extensive use of the language and actions of folly. Even though the whole play cannot be said to be adequately contained in the idea of folly because there are other interests, Lindsay has made much of the dramatic opportunities offered by folly in terms of language and situations and also at the philosophical level of the ambiguities, some of them evil, in the strategic use of folly.

V

Among the dramatists I have discussed here, Heywood appears to be the most emphatic, extensive, and versatile user of fools and folly. Even though the extent of his use of folly varies in intensity, there is no doubt that the dramatic spectacle of watching someone made a fool of is inherent in most of his plays. In a dramatic context this is made more complex because the audience may be induced to see things differently from the manner in which the characters appear to view one another. Thus though in *A Play of Love* Lover loved is made to look ridiculous by Neither loving nor loved, the mockery puts the Vice in some disfavor with the audience. The presence of other characters on the stage during the scene may contribute toward its effectiveness in a positive way, or it may be that they help by their comments and attitudes to broaden the concept of folly so that it becomes a critique of the whole of society, as seems to be the intent in *The Play of the Wether* with its deliberately chosen wide variety of characters from different social levels. In this way Heywood seems near to the use of folly that was found in the *sotties*. He may have been influenced by the precedent set by Skelton with Fansy and Foly in *Magnyfycence*, though he does not follow the same route as Skelton inasmuch as he brings no fool in a professional capacity onto the stage. His direct reference to and departure from French fool plays of different kinds cannot be doubted.

The interrelationships between fools and Heywood's two named Vices are problematic. In many ways they share material, attitudes, and even their approach to other characters. It is probably unwise to try to be too precise in distinguishing between them in Heywood's time, but we may be safe to indicate that for Heywood folly was not necessarily concerned with a purely or exclusively moral evaluation of human behavior, whereas the Vice in the period after the two early examples by this playwright became much more associated with a process of seduction, or temptation, or merely pointing out the nature of moral evil which he in his peculiar way embodied as a presence in many plays. Much of what is foolish in Heywood's characters is not actually wicked.

In plays written only a few years after the publication of Heywood's dramas, Bale came much closer to making the Vices essentially evil. Albeit their evil is seen in ideological terms, his Sedition (*King Johan*) and Infidelity (*Three Laws*) have none of the innocence which we have found to be part of Heywood's concept of folly. Even if they do seem somewhat akin to the fools of festive entertainment, there is no doubting their destructive intention.

In the other plays reviewed we can see the presence of the idea of the jester as provider of festive entertainment and the possibility that the fool, though foolish, may speak agonizing and unpalatable truths. But perhaps the most interesting variant is Lindsay's clever use of the idea of folly as a means of protection in a dangerous political climate. Even though Foly is a rather antipathetic figure, his attack upon abuses was likely to receive concurrence, and if not it may have been dismissed as madness, or perversity, or indeed given the indulgence conventional to the licensed fool. This suggests that folly may generate many different kinds of laughter and that mockery undertaken by fools may be directed at their victims, the befooled; it may reflect upon themselves (*moccum moccabitur*); and it may reflect upon the audience in a world of universal folly where the number of fools is infinite.

The nature of the stage fools under consideration here does not seem to require a formulaic summing up. It appears that some dramatists at least were becoming more and more aware of their potential. However, the inheritance from non-dramatic fools was so diverse and paradoxical that putting them on the stage could be governed directly by theatrical function as well as by the particular interpretation of folly which the dramatists felt suited the intellectual and perhaps emotional objectives of their piece of entertainment and instruction. Both humanism and the reformation altered the philosophical climate, perhaps most significantly towards a more vigorous critique of values in religion, morality, and the state. Fools on stage with all their ambiguity gave immense opportunities for these new uncertainties to be exploited. Further, changes in the idea of the play which meant that different sorts of acting companies could present different types of material must also have been influential. The development of the interlude after 1500 is a manifestation of a new theatrical ambition and indeed confidence, and resources were made more and more available for those wanting to put on plays.

To the above I think we should add that the invention of printing began in the first half of the sixteenth century at last to have an effect upon the dissemination and understanding of plays. Publication may not have been simply a matter of making texts available to more and more actors and companies: it may rather have been a deliberate political act. There seems little doubt that this was the case for Heywood in 1533 and 1534, and for Lindsay much later, as noted above. Bale was very careful about the printing of some of his dramatic texts in 1547 and 1548, and the timing, just at the point of Edward's accession, was politically significant.

Such developments provided scope for the development of folly on the English stage. The examples that we have, even though few, are recognizably manifestations of the currency of Folly, not to mention the benefits to which she herself laid claim.

NOTES

[1] For suggestions about the actual presence of a fool in *Mankind*, see Sandra Billington, "'Suffer Fools Gladly': The Fool in Medieval England and the Play *Mankind*," in *The Fool and the Trickster: Studies in Honour of Enid Welsford*, ed. P. V. A. Williams (Cambridge: D. S. Brewer, 1979), pp. 46–47, and Clifford Davidson, *Visualizing the Moral Life: Medieval Iconography and the Macro Moralities* (New York: AMS Press, 1989), pp. 26–28.

The present study is in part a follow-up of my "Fansy and Foly: The Drama of Fools in *Magnyfycence*," *Comparative Drama*, 27 (1993–94), 426–52.

[2] See E. M. Welsford, *The Fool: His Social and Literary History* (London: Faber and Faber, 1935), pp. 113–27, esp. 114; Sandra Billington, *A Social History of The Fool* (Brighton: Harvester Press, 1984), p. 1.

[3] For the observation that dramatists at the beginning of the sixteenth century had hardly begun to see the moral possibilities in the fool's entertainment, see Victor Bourgy, *Le Bouffon sur la Scène Anglaise au XVIe Siècle* (Paris: O.C.D.L., 1969), p. 487.

[4] See Clifford Davidson, *Illustrations of the Stage and Acting in England to 1580* (Kalamazoo: Medieval Institute Publications, 1991), figs. 75–78, for relevant illustrations from psalters. See also D. J. Gifford, "Iconographical Notes towards a Definition of the Medieval Fool," in *The Fool and the Trickster*, ed. Williams, pp. 18–39.

[5] Olga Anna Dull, *Folie et Rhétorique dans la Sottie* (Geneva: Droz, 1994), pp. 49–54.

[6] Alexander Barclay, *The Ship of Fools*, ed. T. H. Jamieson (Edinburgh: William Paterson, 1874), 2 vols.

[7] Michael West, "Skelton and the Renaissance Theme of Folly," *Philological Quarterly*, 50 (1971), 23-35, esp. 29.

[8] Walter Kaiser, *Praisers of Folly* (London: Victor Gollancz, 1964), pp. 29–30.

[9] Heather Arden suggests that the *sotties* were most successful in the years 1460–1540 (*Fools' Plays: A Study of Satire in the* Sottie [Cambridge: Cambridge Univ. Press, 1980], p. 14).

[10] On earth "we shall see nothing happy and gay unless I've made it so" (Desiderius Erasmus, *Praise of Folly*, trans. Betty Radice [Harmondsworth: Penguin, 1971], p. 87). Dull shows that the shift in emphasis might be derived from Nominalism (*Folie et Rhétorique*, pp. 61–66).

[11] Barbara Swain, *Fools and Folly during the Middle Ages and the Renaissance* (New York: Columbia Univ. Press, 1932), p. 153.

[12] Happé, "Fansy and Foly," pp. 429–32.

[13] In an important discussion of the stage fool in the Rhetoricians' plays, W. M. H. Hummelen notes that the fool in these plays remains entirely separate from the Sinnekens and that his relation to the main action may be one of deep involvement ranging to one of entirely separated commentary (*De Sinnekens in het Rederijkersdrama* [Groningen: J. B. Wolters, 1958], pp. 383–97, esp. 384); he shows that at times on the Dutch stage the fool had a *marot* and hobby horse. See also W. N. M. Hüsken, "The Fool as Social Critic: The Case of Dutch Rhetoricians' Drama," in the present volume, for further analysis of the Dutch stage fool.

[14] For commentary suggesting that the *sotties* translated the aspirations of a

rising class, see Jean-Claude Aubailly, *Le Monologue, le Dialogue et la Sottie* (Paris: Champion, 1976), p. 460.

[15] For a summary of characteristics of fool behavior on stage, see Olive Mary Busby, *Studies in the Development of the Fool in Elizabethan Drama* (Oxford: Oxford Univ. Press, 1923), pp. 63–83.

[16] References are to *The Plays of John Heywood*, ed. Richard Axton and Peter Happé (Cambridge: D. S. Brewer, 1991).

[17] Joel B. Altman, *The Tudor Play of Mind* (Berkeley and Los Angeles: Univ. of California Press, 1978), p. 108.

[18] Thierry Boucquey observes that in France though folly was unable to be part of reason in the *Fête des Fous*, things changed when the fool went on stage (*Mirages de la Farce: Fête de Fous dans Breughel et Molière* [Amsterdam: Benjamins, 1991], pp. 11, 31). Boucquey also draws attention to the meaning of *folie* as madness; cf. Roberta Mullini, *Corruttore di Parole: il Fool nel teatro di Shakespeare* (Bologna: CLUEB, 1983), pp. 11–12, who additionally notes that madness may bring about alteration in the function of language (p. 24).

[19] Dull, *Folie et Rhétorique*, pp. 49–54.

[20] Fourteen lines of this play are preserved in *The Autobiography of Thomas Whythorne*, ed. James M. Osborn (Oxford: Oxford Univ. Press, 1961), pp. 73–74; quoted in Axton and Happé, eds., *The Plays of John Heywood*, p. 309.

[21] "The Epicurean," in *The Colloquies of Erasmus*, trans. Craig R. Thompson (Chicago: Chicago Univ. Press, 1965), p. 541.

[22] See ibid., pp. 220–21.

[23] In these matters Heywood is close to Thomas More, *The Confutation of Tyndale's Answer*, written in 1531 and published by William Rastell in 1532 and 1533: "he promyseth rewarde in heven in sondry playne places of scrypture, for good wurkes done here in erth" (*Yale Edition of the Complete Works of St Thomas More* [New Haven: Yale Univ. Press, 1963–], VIII, Pt. 1, 402).

[24] See W. R. Streitberger, *Court Revels, 1485–1559* (Toronto: Univ. of Toronto Press, 1994), pp. 280 (for 1539), 294 (1553), 299 (1559), and the discussion in Axton and Happé, eds., *The Plays of John Heywood*, pp. 6–10. It is also noteworthy that there is no hint of doubling in any of the extant texts.

[25] Louis Auguste Martin, *Les Ioyeusetez Facecies et Folastres Imaginacions de Caresme Prenant* (Paris, 1830), XIV, Pt. 3. Karl Young, "The Influence of French farce upon the plays of John Heywood," *Modern Philology*, 2 (1904), 1–28, probably overestimated Heywood's borrowings, but Ian Maxwell, though modifying his estimates, accepts that there was a significant debt (*French Farce and John Heywood* [Melbourne: Melbourne Univ. Press, 1946], p. 95).

[26] Martin, *Les Ioyeusetez Facecies et Folastres Imaginacions*, p. 27.

[27] Ibid., p. 28.

[28] Ibid., p. 28.

[29] Ibid., p. 29.

[30] Ibid., p. 42.

[31] The copintank may be anticipated by Barclay: "Do on your Decke Slut: if ye purpos to come oft/ I mean your Copyntanke: And if it wyl do no goode/ To kepe you from the rayne, ye shal have a foles hode" (*Ship of Fools*, I, 38).

[32] Review of Arden, *Fools' Plays*, in *Treteaux*, 2 , No. 2 (1980), 37.

[33] Maxwell, *French Farce and John Heywood*, pp. 74–79. For the text, see *Receuil des Farces, 1450–1550*, ed. A. Tissier (Geneva: Droz, 1989), V, 229–73. Both begin with blessing and homily, and both end with "a mischief on you"; both Pardoners are newly arrived; both expect a humble approach and offerings; both Pardoner and Triacleur offer antidotes for poisoning; the Pardonneur and Friar try to act superior, while the Triacleur and the Pardoner resist.

[34] *La farce d'un Pardonneur, d'un Triacleur et d'une Taverniere*, ll. 106–06. In his note Tissier points out that the St. Anthony pig also turns up in *Pasté*, l. 12.

[35] Note "folyshe friar," l. 213; "a daw," l. 356; "pull the frere downe lyke a fole," l. 513.

[36] The stage direction at l. 467 instructing the Poticary to hop, followed by the wordplay on the word, may link with hopping for a ring as a sign of folly; see note on this line in Axton and Happé, eds., *The Plays of John Heywood*, p. 255.

[37] I.e., *Le Pardonneur, le Triacleur et la Tavernière*; see n. 33, above.

[38] See T. W. Craik, "The True Source of John Heywood's Johan Johan," *Modern Language Review*, 45 (1950), 289–95.

[39] Cf. "woodcock" in *A Play of Love*, as noted above.

[40] These items are to be found in *Icaromennippus* and *Bis Accusatus*—e.g., "and the farmers were praying for rain while the washerwomen were praying for sunshine" (*Icaromennipus* 25, in *Lucian*, trans. A. M. Harmon, Loeb Classical Library (London: Heinemann, 1968), II, 311. The debt was first noted by K. W. Cameron, *John Heywood's "Play of the Wether"* (Ralegh, N.C.: Thistle Press, 1941), pp. 22–26.

[41] Maxwell, *French Farce and John Heywood*, pp. 83–84; see the texts in *Receuil Général des Sotties*, ed. E. Picot (Paris: Firmin Didot, 1902–12), Nos. 23 and 25.

[42] See Greg Walker, *Plays of Persuasion* (Cambridge: Cambridge Univ. Press, 1991), pp. 154–68.

[43] Jupiter's reference to "our hye parlyament" (l. 22) may echo Jupiter's Parliament in Gringoire's *Prince des Sots*, which was also known by Lindsay; see A. J. Mill, "The Influence of Continental Drama on Lyndsay's *Satyre of the Thrie Estaitis*," *Modern Language Review*, 25 (1930), 425–42. But the summoning of what became the Reformation Parliament in 1529 could also have been an issue Heywood wished to address. Walker notes the strength of anti-clerical moves in Parliament in 1529 (*Plays of Persuasion*, pp. 161–62).

[44] Walker, *Plays of Persuasion*, pp. 102–22. For the text see *A New Enterlude of Godly Queen Hester*, ed. W. W. Greg, Materialien zur Kunde des älteren Englischen Dramas, 5 (Leuven: A. Uystpruyst, 1904); I have slightly adapted this text to modern conventions and punctuation in my quotations from it.

[45] Greg adduces a parallel between the smith who made the bull of brass for Phalaris and Aman in Barclay's *Ship of Fools* (II, 39–40); see his note to l. 1030.

[46] Manuscript dated c.1546, and published at Cologne in 1548: see *The Life and Poems of Nicholas Grimald*, ed. and trans. L. R. Merrill, Yale Studies in English, 69 (New Haven: Yale Univ. Press, 1925), pp. 217–357.

[47] John Redford, *Wit and Science*, ed. Arthur Brown, Malone Society (Oxford: Oxford Univ. Press, 1951), p. xi.

[48] According to Mill, Lindsay was in France in 1531, 1532, 1534, and 1536–37 ("The Influence of Continental Drama," pp. 425–30).

[49] Greg Walker, "Sir David Lindsay's *Ane Satire of the Thrie Estaitis* and the Politics of Reformation," *Scottish Literary Journal*, 16 No. 2 (1989), 5–17.

[50] See my "Staging *Lomme Pecheur* and *The Castle of Perseverance*," *Comparative Drama*, forthcoming.

[51] References are to my edition in *Four Morality Plays* (Harmondsworth: Penguin, 1979), but for much background information I have used Douglas Hamer, ed., *The Works of Sir David Lindsay of the Mount*, Scottish Text Soc., 3rd ser. 1–2, 6, 8 (Edinburgh: W. Blackwood and Sons, 1931–36).

[52] E. K. Chambers, *The Mediaeval Stage* (London: Oxford Univ. Press, 1903), I, 209–10; C. Graf, "Sottise et folie dans la Satire des trois Etats," *Recherches Anglaises et Americaines*, 3 (Strasburg, 1970), 5–21.

[53] Lindsay's commitment to the Protestant cause cannot be doubted since there are too many references to Protestant details. Persuasive supporting evidence lies in the case made by Marie Axton that, on the accession of James VI and I to the English throne in 1603, Lindsay's play was printed in London in support of the new monarch's credentials as a Protestant prince ("*Ane Satyre of the Thrie Eastaits*: The First Edition and its Reception," in *A Day Festival*, ed. Alisoun Gard-

ner-Medwin and Janet Hadley Williams (Aberdeen: Aberdeen Univ. Press, 1990), pp. 21–34.

[54] This link has been investigated by Graf, "Sottise et folie dans la Satire des trois Etats," pp. 25–27, but for details of the French mode see also Aubailly, *Le Monologue, le Dialogue, et la Sottie*, pp. 40–49.

[55] Hamer has noted in his edition that this was a motto of the sociétés of fools (*The Works*, IV, 235).

[56] John J. McGavin, "The Dramatic Prosody of Sir David Lindsay," in *Of Lion and Unicorn: Essays on Anglo-Scottish Literary Relations in Honour of Professor John MacQueen*, ed. R. D. S. Jack and Kevin McGinley (Edinburgh: Quadriga, 1993), pp. 39–66, esp. 54.

[57] Arden, *Fools' Plays*, p. 33. A distribution of hats took place at Tournai in 1499 (Hamer, ed., *Works*, IV, 159). However, Folie is not like the benign *sots* in the *sotties* identified by Alan E. Knight, *Aspects of Genre in Late Medieval French Drama* (Manchester: Manchester Univ. Press, 1983), p. 82.

[58] Sandra Billington points out that at one point Foly attacks "Ilk Christian Prince" for making war, apparently condemning Protestant and Catholic alike ("The Fool and the Moral in English and Scottish Morality Plays," in *Popular Drama in Northern Europe in the Later Middle Ages*, ed. Flemming G. Andersen, Julia McGrew, Tom Pettitt, and Reinhold Schröder [Odense: Odense Univ. Press, 1988], p. 132).

[59] Arden notes the motif of the *sotties* that characters frequently remove outer garments to reveal fools' costumes underneath (*Fools' Plays*, p. 34). See also Aubailly's comments concerning "deshabillement forcé" (*Le Monologue, le Dialogue et la Sottie*, p. 447).

The Fool as Social Critic: The Case of Dutch Rhetoricians' Drama

W. N. M. Hüsken

Fools and Chambers of Rhetoric—literary guilds whose members derived pleasure from practicing the art of poetry among themselves and performing drama in public—had a long-standing tradition of cooperation in the late medieval culture of the Low Countries. Some scholars even have argued that fool guilds, along with religious brotherhoods and archery guilds, might have been among the sources for the origin of the Dutch Chambers of Rhetoric.[1] In a limited number of cases, the names or mottoes of some of the companies active in the fifteenth and sixteenth centuries—for example, the "Plompkens" ("Clumsy Fellows") of Arnemuiden or St. Barbara of Kortrijk (Courtrai) with its motto "Godt voedt veel sotten" ("God feeds many fools") —do indeed suggest some sort of relationship with folly.[2] However, the political situation between the end of the fourteenth century and the beginning of the sixteenth makes it more likely that the origin of Dutch Chambers of Rhetoric will be found in present-day northern France. For between 1435 and 1482, Picardy belonged to the Low Countries, whereas Artois, the land north of Picardy including Arras and Lille, had already fallen into the hands of the Burgundians, the official rulers of the Low Countries, fifty years earlier. The Artois area served to connect Flanders, the region in which the Chambers of Rhetoric first became popular as civic or rural literary institutions during the fifteenth century, with French culture. Flanders thus bordered on the home ground of the *Puys*, the companies responsible for, among other things, the performing of mysteries. Therefore the assumption that Dutch Chambers of Rhetoric were modeled on the French *Puys* rather than on archery associations, religious brotherhoods, or fool guilds becomes ever so likely, though we must not deny some influence from these groups as well.[3]

Whatever relationship existed between fools and Chambers of Rhetoric during the first decades of the development of these literary societies, the fact is that fools were active in Chambers as early as the fifteenth century. Fools not only performed in plays but they served a specific function within the companies. Especially during drama competitions, such as the *Landjuwelen* held by the Chambers of Rhetoric from the province of Brabant, fools had their own place in the procession at the official entry into the organizing town. In 1561, when Antwerp hosted one of the most famous *Landjuwelen* ever, the train of the organizing Chamber of Rhetoric, "De Violieren" ("The Stock Flower"), was headed by Duffel, the private fool of Antoon van Stralen (1521–68), dean of the Chamber and one of the Lord Mayors of Antwerp. Juerken, the Chamber's fool, rode on horseback, escorted by two other fools, one of them playing a violin, the other trying to play music on a jawbone and thus visualizing a proverb meaning "to cheat or to misappropriate something" (fig. 9).[4] He and his colleagues from other Chambers of Rhetoric had their own mottoes, proving their utter folly. Juerken's read: "Ick ben soo fray ick en kenne my selven niet" ("I am so handsome I do not know myself"). While proclaiming such slogans to the crowd, the fools tried to stir its laughter. Mechelen's fool, for example, asked "Waer kyckt den zot?" ("Where does the fool look?"), which he himself answered: "Wtter mouwe" ("From out of the sleeve," meaning "to show oneself in one's true colors"). A fool from Breda's Chamber, entering with a cat on the palm of his hand, said: "Ick hebse vonden" ("I have found her").

Fools were also participants in royal entries. Five were present in Joanna of Castille's procession into Brussels in

1496. One of them, entering the town on a stool on horseback, smoked a pipe or blew bubbles (symbolizing vanity), held a bauble in his left hand, and hid a pair of bellows (empty-headedness) behind his back with his right hand (fig. 10). The fact that fools participated in religious, royal, and theatrical processions confirms their general acceptance in all social classes from the highest circles of nobility to the common man. It is therefore not credible to argue that they were considered subversive—at least in their earlier stages of development—for otherwise they would never have been allowed to take a part in these serious events.[5]

Fools were, of course, a large category that would include several sub-types, some of which we would today not associate with the term 'fool.' In everyday life disabled persons were, for example, frequently labeled 'fools.' The mentally handicapped too were regarded as being outside the normal social order or as even less than fully human. Dirc Potter (c.1370–1428), one of the most colorful scribes at the court of Albrecht van Beieren at the Hague, relates an anecdote in his *Blome der Doechden* (*Flower of Virtue*) that was ascribed to Aristotle while in the retinue of Alexander the Great. One day the Emperor found his way blocked by a fool. The guards started beating him in order to clear a passage. But Aristotle, stopping them, said: "He's a fool, not a human being; therefore, he does not need to make way." Yet according to the same author one should avoid their company because their folly was thought to be contagious.[6] While at the end of the medieval period towns did start evicting such "natural" fools, until c.1550 local authorities clearly felt a certain responsibility towards them. In town records we consequently find many entries describing small donations for their food or clothing. The first officially "appointed" town fool ("zot vander stede") is believed to have appeared at the beginning of the sixteenth century. In Bruges, four fools were employed to participate in the Corpus Christi Procession of 1545. As late as 1574, at the time of the same festival, four female fools were given new shoes.[7] But a change of attitude toward fools had slowly become noticeable already after the publication in 1494 of Sebastian Brant's *Narrenschiff* (*Ship of Fools*), which explicitly associates folly with sin. Hence their social position gradually was eroded. This is not to say that their place in society had ever been enviable, for even though mentally deficient fools had enjoyed a certain sympathy during the Middle Ages, we know their treatment was not always very humanitarian. After all, people generally saw them as scapegoats rather than as pitifully poor citizens.[8]

On the stages of the rhetoricians various kinds of fools frequently made their entry, and these included not only those who were born fools but also the slightly mentally deprived and, of course, those who adopted folly as a role to be played. A fourth category may be added, for some stage characters may be considered fools even though their function within the play is entirely different. Such is the case, for example, with peasants in late sixteenth- and early seventeenth-century drama. At the time, civic audiences would regard themselves as more sophisticated than the peasants who lived in rural areas—that is, they viewed them as being fools—hence the impression of foolishness made by peasants time and again in Dutch rhetoricians' drama. For purposes of the present study this last-mentioned category and the mentally deficient will be omitted from our discussion of fools in rhetoricians' drama. The other types of fools do play an extremely important role as stage characters, especially in performances which aim at satirizing specific defects in society. In virtually all cases these fools criticize examples of behavior regarded as unworthy of imitation either by ridicule or, to a lesser degree, by displaying such conduct themselves. A survey of a wide variety of pre-Renaissance Dutch plays containing fools will provide a valuable picture of this figure of entertainment and satire who might range from the natural fool to the artificial fool who in full consciousness played the role of one.

In the following pages I will attempt in part to systematize the function of fools' performances in rhetoricians' drama. Yet even more importantly I wish to provide a view of Dutch culture with its rich dramatic heritage prior to the Renaissance by reviewing a number of the most interesting plays in which fools appear on stage.

I

From the period prior to the sixteenth century Dutch drama has only few surviving play texts. The so-called *Handschrift Van Hulthem*, a manuscript dating back to the beginning of the fifteenth century, includes four *abele spelen* and six *sotternieën*. Except for the *Spel van den Winter ende vanden Somer* (*Play of Winter and Summer*), all these *abele spelen* breath a chivalrous atmosphere. Setting aside a small number of thirteenth-century plays from northern France, they constitute the oldest group of vernacular secular plays in Europe. The six *sotternieën* have nothing to do with fools, despite what their genre designation may suggest (cf. Fr. *sot*). However, folly certainly is a central element of these plays. They show how a stupid man is tricked by a quack (*De Buskenblaser* [*The Blower in the Box*]), by an adulterous woman (*Lippijn*), or by a bossy mother-in-law (*Rubben*), or they show how farmers' wives succeed in outwitting a female outcast whom they accuse of witchcraft (*Die Hexe* [*The Witch*]). The aim of these plays seems to be to convince the audience that topsy-turvy or upside-down power relations, whether at home or in one's vocation, can only lead to chaos.

A second early play, perhaps dating back to 1436, on the battle between summer and winter, a fragment of which is extant at the University Library at Ghent, does include a fool.[9] The fool, opening this *Spel van den Somer ende van den Winter*, is astounded at the large number of people on the roads. He inquires the reason for this from a bailiff, who chases him away. While thus far he has appeared to be relatively normal—his first speech of only fourteen lines is nonetheless quite witty—the irrationality of his reasoning quickly emerges, as in the following inept remark: "Ic sie wel, haddic langhe ghelet, || Men hadt my niet commen seggen thuus" ("I see very well; had I waited a little longer, they would not have ordered me to return home"). The remainder of the text mainly consists of a dialogue between a poor wretch, suffering from the cold winter, and a rich miser who does not want to know anything of charity.

We are permitted to believe that during the fifteenth century many other performances with fools on stage must have existed. Unfortunately, records referring to theatrical activity do not provide explicit evidence but mainly give rather vague descriptions of the plays. Only in very rare instances do the dramatic records reveal something of the contents of the plays. In 1395 and 1419 at Arnhem there were performances of a "her Nyterts spil"; this was a play which may be connected with the German tradition of *Neidhart* texts, the first dramatic representation of which is the *Sankt Pauler Neidhartspiel* from the second half of the fourteenth century.[10] Another play, entitled *Van Lysken dat sie enen man hebben wolde die nae den harnasche roeke* (*Of Lizzy who wanted to have a husband who would smell after a suit of armor*) and obviously comic in character, was performed in 1470 in Deventer.[11] Folly undoubtedly was a central element in these two plays, but we do not know whether they also contained any fools.

After the *Spel van den Somer ende van den Winter* we will need to wait until the beginning of the sixteenth century before encountering a fool in the text of a play that most likely had been presented on the Dutch rhetoricians' stages. The first example that calls itself to our attention is a very remarkable one, and it is equally important as well for the character type that the fool will play in subsequent sixteenth-century drama of the Low Countries. The significance of *Van Nyeuvont, Loosheit ende Practike: hoe sij Vrou Lortse verheffen* (*Of New Findings, Cunning, and Slyness, how they exalt Lady Fraud*)[12] becomes evident when we see that it was published between 1497 and 1501, when publishers were still experimenting with the newly invented device of the printing press, for only those literary texts that would guarantee substantial public interest were put into print. Two of the most important Dutch plays of the fifteenth century, *Lanseloet van Denemerken* (c.1486) and *Elckerlyc* (c.1494), had been issued first, immediately followed by the publication of *Van Nyeuvont, Loosheit ende Practike.*

II

Van Nyeuvont, Loosheit ende Practike merits careful attention. This play and the others published at the turn of the sixteenth century were issued not on account of their dramatic character but rather because printers thought the text of sufficient significance to be read by individual readers, who might include a wider audience than those who would encounter the story only through public recitation or performance. Since the text is meant to be read, narrative passages are included, varying from short introductory remarks to extensive chapter titles summarizing the gist of what is going to follow. Known as a process of *dérimage* ('un-rhyming'), texts which were conceived originally as plays reappeared as chapbooks. This may have been the case with the example of *Mariken van Nieumeghen* (c.1511), a miracle play on the seduction of a simple country girl by the devil and her eventual conversion. However, in this case we are not quite certain whether a narrative version of the story, presented in English translation in *Mary of Nemmegen* of c.1518, preceded the Dutch dramatic version. The question remains a highly debated issue among scholars of Dutch drama, especially since it is known that previously existing narratives did find their way onto the stage. In 1412–13, for example, a performance took place in Bruges of a play on the story of *Amis and Amiloun*, a tale retold time and again after it had first been written down by Radulfus Tortarius, a monk at Fleury who lived at the end of the eleventh century.[13] In 1483, a Dutch adaptation of the French twelfth-century love story *Floris and Blanche-*

flour was dramatized for the stage and performed in Deinze.[14]

During the first half of the sixteenth century, many prose narratives that appeared in print in the Low Countries contained passages in dialogue. Thus prose narratives more and more resembled drama. *Van Nyeuvont, Loosheit ende Practike* likewise is a text that combines verse dialogue and prose, but its use of narrative passages is very limited. Four out the five "chapters" are rounded off with a short narrative preview of what is going to happen next. Since the information supplied by these narrative passages is absolutely superfluous, the text clearly shows its associations with the actual stage. This is fortuitous, since we thus are able to proceed with confidence that the fool included in the play is in fact a stage fool of a type associated with late medieval Dutch drama.

Nyeuvont is a woman who takes pride in being able to maintain herself even in bad times. The literal meaning of her name is "(yet) another shrewd invention." To two lawyers who side with her, "Practijcke" ("Cunning") and "Loosheyt" ("Slyness"), she indicates that she intends to gain absolute power over man, and to reach that goal she will invent a saint, hitherto venerated by only few people, so as to obtain large amounts of money from those who will buy indulgences. The new saint will be called "Sinte Lorts," and it is her hope that thousands of believers will visit her (movable!) shrine and subscribe to her guild. Practijcke employs "Hardt van Waerseggen" ("Untruthfulness") and his valet "Cleyn Vreese" ("Fearing Little") to carry the shrine throughout the country (fig. 11). The name of the "new" saint is derived from the verb "lortsen," meaning to perpetrate fraud. The author, however, was less interested in the sale of indulgences than in humans' love of luxuries which was expressed in the ever increasing abundance of clothing especially by those who could not afford such expensive garments. From the outset this vice is criticized by a fool, "Schoontooch" ("Glamor"), although it is his *marot* (bauble) "Quaet en Waerseggen" ("Backbiter Telling

Truths") which whispers various things into his ears. Of course it is the seemingly innocent fool himself who reports his words to us:

> Ow hoort mij*n* marote god bedroef haer muylgat
> Sy seyt dat alte menich verrompen vuylvat
> Met ghehuerde cleedere*n* frisch en moy sijn
> En*de* op ghespoelt naden nyewen toy sijn
> Maer dese en sijn in sinte Lorts niet gheouwen[15]

> (Ay, hear my bauble, God damn her snout. She says, too many a wrinkled trash-bag looks fresh and fine in rented clothes which are polished up after the latest trappings. But these are not included in St. Lorts' guild.)

The play, being one of the earliest extant Dutch texts containing a fool, shows an extensive use of interaction between fool and bauble in a manner which becomes conventional thereafter in the sixteenth century. Threatening to silence his bauble—eventually he will give his *marot* a few blows on his nose: "hodt dat || Swijcht noch oft ghi crijcht noch een faetse"[16] ("Take that! Be silent now or else you will receive another blow")—the fool tells the audience what his comrade had confided to him. He also expands on its waggish remarks by asking, as if surprised, for further explanation. Thus he too becomes a critic of society and seems plainly to convey his own thoughts without being required to take personal responsibility for them:

> Tsus marote. oft ic stoot v door v kele
> Ghi sijt metten mele / van tuyl bestouen
> Swijcht oft ic clop v op uwen bach ouen
> God bedroef uwen snatre / vuyl sassem kemele
> Segdij dat Meest elc sijnde onder de*n* hemele
> In sijn neringhe soect lortssinghe en*de* sueringhe
> Ey leelike tremasschele hi en doet noch lueringhe
> Maer hi es ghetrouwe in sijn wandelinghe
> Somen daghelijcs sien mach aen sijn ha*n*delinghe
> Doet hijs niet. vuyl bacpanne / ghi liechter om.[17]

> (Shush, bauble or else I will cut your throat. You are all powdered with Tuyl's flour [i.e., you are crazy]. Be silent or I will

> knock on your baking oven [i.e., mouth]. God damn your beak, fowl disgusting camel. Are you telling me that every man living under heaven's skies is looking for fraud and corruption in his trade? Ay, ugly face, he does not do any wrong, but he is trustworthy in his behavior as one can see every day in his actions. Doesn't he? Well, dirty frying pan, you are lying!)

There are suggestions in the text to indicate that the actor playing the role of the fool either was a ventriloquist or otherwise distorted his voice to sound as though it might be the bauble speaking, for in many instances Schoontooch's words prove to be a reaction to a preceding statement by Quaet en Waerseggen. We only realize that it is the bauble who is supposedly speaking when its words are followed by a reprimand by the fool (ll. 196–200, 210–14, 456–65). The bauble's comment is overheard by other characters in the play who occasionally react to it. At a certain moment, Cleyn Vreese sighs: "Ick wou die marote nv laghe int water plat || Al soudse verdrincke*n*/ ken staker niet een ha*n*t an" ("I wish that bauble were lying in the water now. Even if it should drown, I would not reach out my hand to it").[18] In one case a stage direction (l. 195) even indicates that fool and bauble are speaking simultaneously! The play ends in a report to Nyeuvont by Loosheyt and Practijke of the great success they have achieved in bringing Vrou Lorts to the public's attention.

The published play caused the figure of Vrou Lorts to be tremendously popular with the public at large, as witness other literary texts containing this character. In a mock-sermon, *Sinte Reyn-uyt* ("St. Squanderer"), patron saint of all wasters, Reyn-uyt's mother is identified as Vrou Lorts, whose appearance in this genre is not surprising. The mock sermon tended to absorb similar satirical figures, including St. Nemo, St. Raisin, St. Herring, St. Onion, and other fake "saints"—figures in these French and Dutch *sermons burlesques* which made fun of the veneration of various questionable saints.

Vrou Lorts also would appear on stage in a play of 1565 by the Haarlem playwright Louris Jansz which was included in the massive drama collection from *Trou Moet Blijcken* (*Loyalty Should be Proved*), the Chamber of Rhetoric from the same town.[19] In this play, Vrou Lorts advises "Tgemeen volck" ("Common People") to borrow money to purchase goods with a view to allowing him to sell them at a profit. If the plan fails the man has still the option of having himself officially declared bankrupt.

At the end of the sixteenth and the beginning of the seventeenth century, Vrou Lorts had not been forgotten. In 1596, a "wedding" was celebrated in Leiden between Vrou Lors and "Joncker Mors" ("Master Grubby"). The event was meant to encourage contributions to a lottery being held to finance the building of a hospice for patients suffering either from plague or from mental diseases. Initiated by Pieter Cornelisz van der Mersch (or Morsch) alias Piero, the fool of "De Witte Acoleyen" ("The White Columbines"), the festival was organized in the manner of a *Landjuweel* or drama competition between various Chambers of Rhetoric. A selection of the poems that had been recited was printed and, of course, sold to serve the same charitable purpose.[20] The meaning of the name "Vrou Lorts" has now, however, changed because here it refers to a specific type of frumpish woman. The same connotation is found in later publications, as when she is mentioned in a songbook *Den Bloem-hof van de Nederlantsche Ieught* (1608) and in a play by one of the leading Amsterdam authors of the early seventeenth century, Samuel Coster's *Tiisken van der Schilden* (1613). The best-known comedy writer of the time, G. A. Bredero (1585–1618), applies yet another meaning to the name in his *Moortje* (1616) when he views Juffrouw Lors as the equivalent of a female miser.

III

On 20–27 July 1551 Brussels was the site of a festival of fools. The Burgundian capital may have been very hospitable to fools, for as early as 1446 the Mechelen town records mention a "ghemaecten abd van bruessele die hier toten bisscop van St. Rom[bout] comen was" ("sham abbot from Brussels who had come here to visit the bishop of St. Rombout's church").[21] The celebrations under discussion here, like the ones from Leiden 1596 discussed above, were modeled on the *Landjuwelen* of Brabant. Hence prizes were given for individual and group entertainments, varying from the most hilarious entry in a procession to the best farce in performance. The event was initiated by a local painter, Jan Colyns alias Walravens, an unattractive and short hunchback whose nickname was Oomken. Literally, the name means "little uncle," but, as in English, it also embraces the slang expression for a pawnbroker's shop. Oomken ruled from an elevated stage and judged the alleged "crimes" of his fellow fools. The same stage was, of course, used for performing plays as well. A description of what happened during the eight days Brussels saw itself inundated by fools—upon their invasion of the town, their silly frolic was seen everywhere, and hundreds came from neighboring towns to witness the unique event—was left behind in a contemporary chronicle.[22] On the second day, which was a Tuesday, the fools set out to attend Mass in St. Goedele's Church with Oomken as their leader riding on a small donkey. The service included songs by a choir "jn discante" ("off key"). The event reminds us of the ancient *asinaria festa*, the well-known Feast of Fools or, rather, "Feast of Asses." The actual competition also included a tournament on hobby horses made of wickerwork. Fools from Lille and Valenciennes proved to be the most successful competitors.

Presumably on the first day of the event, Oomken promulgated the statutes of the newly established Empire of Fools which were published in Louvain in 1552: *Den Eedt van Meester Oom met vier Ooren, Prince der Dooren* (*The Oath of Master Uncle, Prince of Fools, with four Ears*).[23] The *Eedt* resembles a play in so far as its text is divided over three different roles: a clerk, a king, and the audience. On the king's behalf, the clerk summons the audience to pay attention to the following writ. All present will have to swear an oath promising to obey the new king. This means they will have to protect

> alle geestelicke personen
> Die gheern onder d'oude cleermerct woonen
> En gheern in den boec lesen tot hunder schade
> Die men open slaet niet wijs van rade,
> Die wijn en bier niet en laten verscalen
> En veel meer borghen dan si connen betalen,
> Nonnen die uutlopen en gaen hun gangen,
> Munneken die de cappe op den tuyn hangen,
> Dese moetij al scutten en schermen
> Als si van aermoede claghen en kermen.[24]

(all religious persons who happily live under the old clothes square and who, to their own detriment, love to read in the book which they foolishly open. Who do not allow beer and wine to go stale and who borrow much more than they can pay for. Eloping nuns going their own way, monks hanging their cowls over the fence—all these you must protect and shield when, out of poverty, they start complaining and moaning.)

Other groups eligible for protection by the fools are braggart soldiers and noble knights on rented horses, promiscuous women and matchmakers, vagabonds and millers without a mill, merchants, quack doctors, brewers, innkeepers, sailors, weavers, and a dozen or more other representatives of various professions, all without exception heading for "Sinte Reynuut" (St. Squanderer). The list even includes rhetoricians, musicians, artists, and lawyers. All have to eat and drink till midnight and sleep well into the day. Whoever asks them to do any labor shall be expelled from the Empire of Fools. The king is invited to say yes or no to these articles. Consequently he says: "Jae, jae, neen, neen" ("Yes, yes, no, no"). Next, swearing by a chamberpot, he must put his fingers on the cobblestone growing behind his ear and pronounce an utterly foolish oath. Thereafter the clerk invites all bystanders to cheer the new king: "Vive le Roy stultus stultorum." Finally all present must swear to be loyal to him, each and every one of them saying "yes, no," sticking his finger to his backside, and finally kissing it ("Steckt nu al u vingeren in 't gat en cust se dan").

Meester Oom's popularity extended not only to Brussels alone but also to other Flemish towns. His first documented re-appearance was in Antwerp in 1561 when he participated in the procession of the Brussels Chamber *De Corenbloem* (*The Cornflower*) introducing the city's *Haechspel*, a competition for less important Chambers of Rhetoric that was held immediately after the famous Antwerp *Landjuweel*. Oomken was seated on a chariot lavishly decorated with greenery, draped all around with playing-cards; he proclaimed: "Ick come oock opt Haech-Spel" ("I too will attend the *Haechspel*"). At Easter 1572, he participated in one of Mechelen's annual processions, the "Peisprocessie." In this case the town records refer to him as "Oom, geck van brucelle met zynen sone" ("Uncle, Brussels' fool, and his son").

IV

One of the many sub-genres of Dutch rhetoricians' drama consists of plays performed during dinner—hence *tafelspelen*, or dinner plays. These plays differ from those performed outdoors on a stage, especially in the way that the audience is addressed, for the persons who were eating and drinking would be suddenly transformed, sometimes without warning, into spectators at a performance. Because of the limited space available for performing drama between the tables, the number of characters in this kind of play was necessarily small, usually between one and four characters. Doubling, a possible solution for expanding the number of characters (as is the case, for example, in English interludes), is not used as a device in *tafelspelen*.

In some of these plays one character in fact carries the entire plot: a peasant's wife trying to sell eggs, a quack putting up his booth and attempting to sell some of his merchandise, a soldier boasting about his courage, a fool playing with his bauble. In each only a few stage properties would appear. At times the audience was brought into the performance, and in these instances it would become in fact a "fictional audience" within the action of the play. The result would be a double transformation, for those sitting at the feast would be changed into spectators, subsequently becoming potential clients of egg sellers and quacks. In other cases characters involved a specific property in their action and hence created a "fictional character" such as the boasting soldier's own shadow. In fools' monologues the important stage property is predictably their bauble.

Fools nevertheless seldom failed to address their monologues directly to their audiences. In the anonymous *Een Marot Sot Geclap*, a hitherto unpublished dinner play from the Haarlem rhetoricians' Chamber "Trou Moet Blijcken,"[25] the fool thus speaks to the "heeren" ("gentlemen") present at a meal without giving any further indication of the reason for their assembly—a feature which perhaps makes the text suitable for different kinds of functions and, consequently, appropriate for repeat performances.[26] However, here the fool's first words are not to the audience but to his bauble, named "Sot Geclap" ("Foolish Chatter"), which he invites to greet the assembly, whereupon he introduces himself as "Soet Geselschap" ("Sweet Company"). The fool, making a rather one-sided use of his single stage prop, listens to his *marot* as it whispers into his ears, whereupon his master passes his remarks on to the spectators. After the two have sung a song, they prepare the presentation of a gift for the audience. Sot Geclap claims their present could be described as a naughty bird in black and white colors. Curious to find out more about this strange gift, Soet Geselschap starts guessing about its identity. The fool lists a dozen and more birds, but without the right answer. Subsequently, *marot* makes his master believe their present is a "cijsken" (siskin). It is, as we might expect, a trick, and in the end Soet Geselschap produces a pair of dice out of *marot*'s hood. Only now is it obvious that a pun has been intended ("cijsken" is a homonym that when spoken sounds like the word referring to dice, "sixes," as well as to the name of a certain bird, a "siskin"). Instead of the (virtually obligatory) moral lesson with which most dinner plays conclude, the author of this *tafelspel* merely wishes his audience to have good fortune ("dat fortuijn u graci wil verlienen"). Advising them to remain in Good Company and leaving their gift behind, fool and bauble take leave of the gentlemen.

In another dinner play, *Een Marot noodt ter Bruijloft* (*A Bauble's Invitation to a Wedding*),[27] in the same Haarlem collection, the fool quickly forgets his bauble after having entered the hall of a merry company—presumably those present at a wedding—and invites them to attend a wedding in Flanders where the Duke of "Mal" ("Folly," but perhaps also referring to Malle or Westmalle, a village near Antwerp) will give in marriage his son "Loeten" ("Lout") to "Dwaeseg die Grijffijn" ("Foolish Talk, the Griffin"; the last word is a deliberate corruption of "gravin" [English: "countess"]). Since all present at the moment are related to the couple, they should, according to the fool, not miss out on this special event. The play is basically a dramatized mock invitation that names all kinds of functionaries at an intended wedding at which a completely different class of people will temporarily govern the world under the rule of folly.

A more conventional way of interacting between fool and bauble is reported in a printed *Tafel-spel van een Parsonagie, een Sot speelende met een Marot* (*Dinner play of one Character, a Fool playing with a Bauble*).[28] Once more the fool and his bauble are present at a wedding. *Marot* refuses to greet the bride and is consequently threatened by his master, who offers to give him a couple of blows. The poor bauble then appears to have soiled his trousers. The monologue culminates in the bauble's licentious description of how the bride's parents generated her:

> haer vaer en moer speelden oock sulcken spel
> Al heten zy Nel t'is haer niet vergeten
> Hoet haer vaerken maecte hy werde niet gesmeten

Als hy haer ginck meten zy aen zy
So wasse bly en lachten daerom
Ick weet niet hoe zijt maeckte zy lagen zo crom
Sy speelde mom mom ick en sie v niet[29]

(her father and mother played such a game too. Even though her name is Nel, she has never forgotten how her father managed to do it. He was not smitten when he started to measure her side by side. Hence she was happy and laughed about it. I do not know how she managed to do it: they were lying so crooked. She played "mum, mum, I don't see you.")

Despite the limitations of the monologue format, fools displayed a wide variety of means of expression in order to depict a dramatic character on stage. Fools either played at communicating with their baubles and their audience, or they had to talk to themselves. The introduction of a bauble as a (fictional) character of course enabled them to create conflict, but it also allowed them to say things no one would ever dare say in one's own voice. However, as soon as a second or a third character joined him on stage, the fool's ways of acting would radically change.

On 29 September 1559, the feast of St. Michael coinciding with a Brussels' feast of fools, the Chamber of Rhetoric "Het Mariacransken" ("The Rosary") performed a play, the *Tafelspel van Twee Sotten* (*Dinner Play of Two Fools*), for the local magistrates. Because of the religiously seditious character of the play, a number of priests had lodged complaints with the authorities. Some of the members of the Chamber that were involved were summoned to defend themselves and to confirm that they were still orthodox and loyal Christians. Franchoys van Ballaer, the alleged author of the play, claimed the text had been part of the Rosary's archives for over sixty years. Hans Leers and Simon Hobossch, the two actors who had played the parts of the "geboren sot" ("Natural Fool") and the "gemaecten sot" ("Artificial Fool") respectively, confirmed his testimony. Eventually the rhetoricians were able to find an old man who had been in the performance of the same play sixty years ago. After so many years he was even capable of quoting large fragments of the text, thus "proving" the members of the Chamber to have spoken the truth. He did not know, of course, how the Brussels rhetoricians had been able to lay their hands on this text. The practice of giving a repeat performance of a successful play after many years was, as the man confirmed, quite customary. It must have been mainly on account of his testimony that the members of the "Mariacransken" were not convicted. By placing this text back in time, the rhetoricians of course intended to free it of any religious subversiveness. Whether or not their claim was true, it was in any case successful.

Did the Brussels clergy have anything like a valid reason in mind for indicting the rhetoricians? The natural fool, looking for his patron, the king, fears the artificial fool, who blocks his way. The latter asks his name and wants to know more about his relatives. The strange answers of the natural fool will enrage the artificial fool:

Den gemaecten sot
hoe heetij soene
Den geboren sot
jc heet icke /
tonsent woent noch een die het men brurken
Den gemaecten sot
hoe heet u vaerken en u murken. . . .
Den geboren sot
murken het murken // vaerken het vaerken[30]

(*The Artificial Fool*:
What's your name, son?
The Natural Fool:
My name is I. At home there is another one whom they call little brother.
The Artificial Fool:
What's the name of your father and mother? . . .
The Natural Fool:
Mother's name is mother, father's is father.)

The artificial fool threatens to put his "mues" ("mouse") —a word that in this context does not seem to make any sense[31]—on the natural fool's shoulders, perhaps implying the act of hitting him with his bauble. The artificial fool takes great pleasure in teasing the poor fellow, whom he forces to kiss his "mues." In a short time the artificial fool calms down and asks the natural fool what things he will bring to the king. "Stones, just stones," says the natural fool, "but people give them different names." This, of course, arouses the artificial fool's interest. Eager to find out what kind of stones his opponent carries, he starts guessing, in each case incorrectly according to the natural fool who only admits that his mother did not allow him to play with them earlier this morning. In the end the precious stones turn out to be communion wafers. Disappointed with the outcome, the artificial fool gives the boy a sound beating. The Brussels priesthood would not surprisingly have been horrified at the sight of the sacrilege of the Host's appearance in a comic play, nor could they have been pleased with a text which suggests that the natural fool's mother is a priest's concubine.

Later in the same year the performance of a second play containing fools, still in Brussels but by a different Chamber of Rhetoric, was also charged with being subversive. Two plays had been performed at the wedding of a certain Jan de Fuytere, senior official in the King's service. The topic of the first drama was not disputed, for it was a moral play on a rich ill person and a poor healthy one, both brought to *Patientia* through confrontation with a Crucifix. The sequel to such moral plays was traditionally a farce, in this case a *Tafelspel van Drie Sotten* (*Dinner play of Three Fools*) that evoked the anger of one of the parish priests of St. Goedele's church. In a prologue, Lady Rhetoric complains about the dishonor bestowed on her art by various critics. A Friend in Distress ("Vrient ter noot") asks why she is lamenting. He denies that her influence is waning and announces the coming of three free lovers ("liefhebbers") of her art who at that moment are approaching to offer their gifts. Enter three fools, an Artificial Fool ("Den gemaicten sot"), a Conceited Fool ("Den opgeblasen sot"), and a Religious Fool ("Den gheestelycken sot"). The first fool is completely wrapped up in playing with his bauble, which he politely greets though in return the doll breaks wind under his nose:

> kyck kyck siet ditte
> heij da heij neen neen so sout best clincken
> Due voe garde / ja sou dat stincke*n*
> Sus so niet meer gij souwet te bont maken[32]

(Look! Look! Watch this! Hey there, hey, no no, thus it would sound best. *Dieu vous garde*. Yes, that would smell horribly! Ho, no more of that. You would go too far.)

On seeing him busy with his bauble, the Conceited Fool starts ridiculing him. The two are interrupted by the third fool, the Religious Fool. Since the last does not wear the traditional outfit of a fool, the Artificial Fool offers him his garment. Outraged, the Conceited Fool asks him whether he does not know who the other man is. The Religious Fool tries to settle him down, but the Artificial Fool continues to give the two others every reason to remain angry with him. Moreover, without any difficulty he guesses their respective names and exposes them as the greatest fools on earth. All of them do everything they can to prove that the others are the greater fools. The Conceited Fool, for example, criticizes the Religious Fool:

> gij wilt ijsraels god doen offerhande
> en gy eerdet gulden calf tuwer scande
> gy beroemt v abrahams gelooue rechuerdich
> en gy versmaet de salighe beloofte weerdich
> gij acht meer op sterre kijckers profecije
> dan op der vier euangelisten bootscap blije
> es dit sotternije of wijsheyt jc vraecht v[33]

(You want to do sacrifice to Israel's God and, to your dishonor, you are honoring the golden calf. You think Abraham's belief to be just and you spurn the blessed worthy promise. You respect astrologers' prophecies more than the four evangelists' joyful message. Is this folly or wisdom, I ask you.)

The central conflict in the play appears between the Conceited Fool and the Religious Fool. The Artificial Fool mostly stands aloof, restricting himself to critical remarks such as: "hier ghebreken twee marotten || haddijer elck eene so soudij te vreden syn" ("Two baubles are missing here. Should each of you have one, you would both be satisfied").[34] Miraculously, the three eventually conclude an armistice and decide to adopt different names. The Artificial Fool will henceforth be known as "rechte verstandighe" ("truly sensible"), whereas the other two will be called "geestelycke wijse" ("religious sage") and "oeijtmoedighe simpele" ("humble simple man"). All three strip off their outer attire to indicate that they have left their former folly behind. In this case, the parish priest of St. Goedele's will merely have felt offended by seeing a religious person being identified with a fool.

These two plays permit a much larger amount of social criticism than the single-actor format of the monologue. The fools especially attack the clergy. A remarkable feature of the *Tafelspel van Drie Sotten* is that the Artificial Fool—the character that should be associated with bells, donkey's ears, multi-colored dress, and bauble—functions as the instigator of a conflict between others and withdraws himself from the actual struggle once he has succeeded in setting it in motion.

V

Fools participate in the stage action in a dozen or more other rhetoricians' plays. All of these cannot be discussed in the present study. Moreover, in some cases their role is so small that there is no reason for detailed analysis. For example, in Job Gommersz's play *De Bedrogen Minnaars* (*The Deceived Lovers*) of 1565, a fool and a man called "Subtijl Bedijeden" ("Subtle Explanation") conclude the play. The story presents three lovers, each arranging a rendezvous with the same woman, who promises to meet them at night in the churchyard. The three are told to disguise as the Devil, Death, and a deceased man in a coffin. Eventually, in the crucial scene, they will frighten each other off during a sequence of actions that are meant to be performed entirely in pantomime.[35] In the end Subtijl Bedijeden and the fool provide an explanation to the audience concerning the meaning of the mime play. Why this explanation was felt to be necessary is difficult to ascertain. The role of the fool is, in any case, fairly conventional: playing with his bauble, he threatens to punish it if it does not behave, etc. Through his presence, the three lovers' behavior is explicitly ridiculed, but his contribution hardly puts the matter in a different perspective.

Another play containing a fool—if the character in this instance is to be thus identified—acting in the margin is provided by the prologue to the fifth play of the *Spelen van die Wercken der Bermherticheyd* (*Plays on the Works of Mercy*).[36] "Sotheyt" ("Folly") is convinced that the world will judge his actions differently as soon as he achieves a reputation for being wise. His strategy of course draws on the absurd, for he arranges to change his clothes with "Wijsheyt" ("Prudence"). "Bekender der Wijsheyt" ("Expert on Prudence"), the first person Sotheyt encounters, provides a test of his supposed transformation. Not unexpectedly, he recognizes Sotheyt's true identity without any difficulty whatsoever. The incident causes Bekender der Wijsheyt to realize that the world must be clearly turned upside down if things like this happen: "Sotheyt doet/ dat Wijsheyt Sotheyt slacht" ("Folly makes Prudence resemble Folly"). Here it is folly rather than the presence of a fool— i.e., Sotheyt's representation of an abstract or allegorical concept instead of a concrete character impersonating foolish behavior—that is central to the play.

An entirely different kind of acting in the margin by a fool is found in *Charon de Helsche Schippere* (*Charon, Hell's Skipper*),[37] a free adaptation, written in 1551, of one of Lucian's dialogues.[38] Briefly summarized, the narrative is as follows. Charon has earned himself a day off from his master Pluto which he intends to use to get acquainted with the world, the place which has been providing him with so many customers for such a long time. Mercury is invited to serve as his guide. In order to be able to oversee the whole world, they place the three highest mountains, Mount Caucasus, Mount Parnassus, and Mount Olympus, one on top of the other. From their high position they see hordes of people, all striving for more power and more wealth. From Charon's perspective they all look like ants. Some are mentioned by name; all of them, of course, are mighty kings and beautiful queens from classical antiquity. However, Charon knows that each of them will eventually appear naked in his boat to be taken across to the underworld. This, finally, is the author's message to the audience.

The play is enriched by addition of a fool named "Nieuloop" ("Newsmonger") to the dialogue. Instead of carrying a bauble, he rides a gray hobby horse named "Clappage" ("Gossip"), which he occasionally has to curb: "we, he, he! peerdeken!" ("Ay, ho, ho! horsy!").[39] The fool rarely enters into contact with the other characters on stage but rather confines himself to commenting on their dialogue. He mainly articulates those thoughts which might have come to the minds of the spectators who are watching the action of the play. As intermediary between characters and the public, he positions himself on the boundary of the stage, perhaps comparable to the way the fool is positioned in the famous engraving of Pieter Bruegel's *Temperantia* (fig. 12). Even the way in which he enters the playing area—i.e., by pushing his way to the stage through the crowd: "Ruymt plaetse, ruymt plaetse, ick muster ooc syn"[40] ("Make way, make way, I have to be there as well") —is symbolic of this marginal position. He frequently combines his astonishment about the events with moralizing comment. An exuberant outburst of laughter by Charon at someone dying from a tile landing on his head, for example, leads to the following reflection by Nieuloop:

> Ey! hoort my datte!
> Dits emmer een werck van vremder aert.
> de hoondere lacht als qualijck vaert;

> de sulcke is blijde in sanders doleren.[41]
>
> (Well! Listen to that! This is truly a work of a strange nature. The scoffer laughs if things go wrong. He rejoices in someone else's misery.)

Occasionally, but still very rarely, do Charon and Mercury react to Nieuloop's remarks: "Sus, clappart, sus," Charon says, "ghy sult noch in myn schip verwarmen, als ghy doot sijt" ("Shush, chatter-box, shush, you will get warm in my boat once you are dead").[42] The fool agrees with Charon and Mercury concerning the foolish world's pursuit of happiness and translates their words into terminology that would be more explicable to a Christian audience. The fee to be paid to the ferry-man thus equals "doechdelijcke wercken" ("works of virtue").

While the author's supplementing of the classical story with a fool is perhaps somewhat surprising in the context of this particular drama, this character's actions are certainly effective. For although his presence on stage is marginal in that Nieuloop merely creates a bridge between the world of the audience and the stage, his remarks are central to the message the play sets out to convey to the public: "Vanitas vanitatum et omnia vanitas." However, the reason for adding a fool to the story may have been a different one. Charon's boat will not have been particularly familiar to the non-classically trained members of the audience, but the author was able to turn this lack of familiarity to good use, since he may have borrowed the fool from a "boat" with which his public was much better acquainted —that is, the Ship of Fools. Moreover, since the symbolism of the Ship in both cases denounces man's worldly striving and advises him to replace folly with a moral life, the imagery is consistent, and the fool in this play is not to be seen as an anomaly.

VI

The fool's conventional way of giving shape to his role in *Van Nyeuvont, Loosheit ende Practike* has been discussed above. An entirely different kind of fool, possibly of an equally early period, appears in a text in a manuscript now preserved in the archives of the Vatican Museum (Rome). The play in this case is entitled *'t Spel van den Spigel* (*The Play of the Mirror*). Two characters, a fool ("Sot") and a youngster ("Jonck"), open the play. Sot reminds his friend of the wedding of a couple to whom they are supposed to present a gift later in the day. Deliberations about what to bring do not take long: they will contribute a mirror. Lacking sufficient funds to buy one, Jonck decides to fetch his mother's looking glass. The fool betrays his hostile character by anticipating his friend's reception and beating at his mother's hands when he is trying to steal her mirror. However, his delight is short-lived when Jonck returns with the mirror within seconds. Sot thereupon takes revenge, or so it seems, by dropping it on the floor. The sight of the broken glass provokes a fight between the two. Enter a woman, "Vreyss van den Doet" ("Fear of Death"), who offers to provide another mirror for them. Elated at their luck, Sot and Jonck invite the woman to share the presentation of their gift. Now the audience is addressed in a way similar to the manner we have seen above in monologues: there is a change from being spectators at a performance into being a celebrating company at the wedding. This seems quite appropriate since the play was presumably written for a wedding in the first place. The nature of the mirror Vreyss van den Doet donates to the married couple is, of course, different from the one that Sot and Jonck intended to bring. Although the text of the play does not precisely define it, the suggestion has been made that it may have been a skull or a pamphlet of the *Ars moriendi* genre.[43]

In contrast to the majority of the fools in the plays discussed above, the fool in *De Spigel* is not the stock character we have come to expect. In fact, he could be replaced by any other character displaying a young and preposterously exaggerated behavior. Meant to complement Jonck, he visualizes the moral defects from which young people suffer. Apart from one or two remarks which betray his somewhat distorted mind, Sot is not a conventional fool. His presence on stage serves a purely teleological goal; he participates in a scheme devised by the author to convey a moral message to the public. While the high-spirited mood of the wedding party is symbolized by the fool, the play's moral statement at its conclusion emphasizes the contrast between these high spirits and the reflective thought with which it ends.

A large number of plays written by Dutch rhetoricians aim in fact at conveying moral lessons, and likewise fools are used frequently to show how inappropriate choices have severe implications, especially when viewed in a religious perspective. For example, the plays often direct their satire at extravagant attire and other aspects of an erring humanity. In other words, characters appear in clothes to display elements that are linked both with a professional group and with fools. Changing one's garment is symbolic of the acceptance of a different attitude, as in *Bruer Willeken,* a play performed in Hasselt, a rural town in the province of Brabant some seventy kilometers east of Brussels, in 1565. The central character of the play is "Halff Verdoelt" ("Halfway Straying"), a monk in a friar's habit under which he is wearing the costume of a fool. Bruer Willeken, a priest but with a large straw hat on his head and a sledgehammer around his neck, allows Halff Verdoelt to become acquainted with the world. Once he has thrown off his habit, Halff Verdoelt is bewildered by the strange costume he is wearing underneath. Soon he meets "Ducht voor Misdoen" ("Fear for Doing Wrong") and "Vreese voor Dende" ("Fear of the End"), a priest and a nun. The play develops into an extensive allegory when these characters at a certain point will find three ladders, which symbolize the three estates which make up the world: Church, Nobility, and the Laboring Classes. Each has seven rungs. The one which belongs to the Church, for example, has prudence, providence, humility, fervor, chastity, constant prayer, and bodily death. Instead of prudence, however, Halff Verdoelt prefers folly! And chastity should, according to him, be replaced by "spelen met amijen" ("playing with women"). Besides, he thinks the ladder too steep. The two other ladders do not please him either, but then he discovers a fourth one lying on the ground. Although it is quite crooked, Halff Verdoelt positions it against the world, presumably a globe placed on the stage. Its steps have names like Sinful Progress, Venom of Virtue, Life of Unease, and the like. As soon as he climbs this ladder, "Catyvighe" ("Miserable") pops out of the globe and, grabbing Halff Verdoelt by his hair, screams that he wants to escape from the world. He severely criticizes the way people treat each other:

> Wie tgoet van den aermen meest can onthouwen,
> Die is meest geacht in swerelt betrapen;
> Wie meest ruckt en pluct aen de schapen,
> Dats ter werelt de meeste prelate;
> Wie meest rooft en schooft voor syn bate,
> Dyen biet men eere tot een somme[44]

(He who is best able to deprive the poor of their goods, is best respected in having power over the world. He who pulls and plucks the sheep, is regarded the best prelate in the world. He who robs and hoards up quantity of goods for his own benefit, is offered greatest honor.)

Grain merchants in particular receive Cathyvighe's scorn. They keep last year's meager harvest in their granaries and as a result the poor must suffer severely. Historically 1565 was a year of disaster with regard to the supply of agricultural products. In 1564, grain prices had been soaring because of small harvests in France. In addition, the Sound in Denmark was closed off at the end of April 1565. Consequently, grain from countries on the Baltic Sea could no longer reach the Low Countries. On 25 September the government announced price restrictions but to no avail. The Hasselt Chamber of Rhetoric proved to be very quick in reacting to the most recent reports from abroad, even quicker than their colleagues from Haarlem who staged a play on the same topic later during this year.[45] The play from Hasselt, however, treats the current situation only at its conclusion. Recent events may have caused the author to revise the play's ending by adapting an older version to the news of the day. In any case, the fool—once more, he is not a traditional one—decides to abandon the idea of going out into the world and instead retreats to his monastery.

Fools who act in a traditional manner with their baubles frequently tell the truth in an extremely blunt way. We have seen that in a number of plays the *marot* serves as the device which openly attacks human defects in the other characters on stage. Typical behavior is exemplified by "Twyffelic Zin" ("Hesitation") and his bauble "Cranc Gheloove" ("Feeble Belief") in Cornelis Everaert's *Spel vanden Nyeuwen Priester* (*Play of the Neophyte*)[46] as well as by "Quaet en Waer" ("Evil and True") with "Swijgen en Dencken" ("Being Silent and Thinking") in *Minckijsers*.[47] Conventional behavior appears implicitly even in "Boerdelick Wesen" ("Funny Nature") and his *marot* in Lambrecht Dirrixsz. de Vult's *Tafelspel van Jonstige Minne en Boerdelick Wesen* (*Dinner Play of Benevolent Love and Funny Nature*)[48] and in the fool and his bauble in *De Sotslach* (*The Fool's Accolade*), one of the funniest sixteenth-century Dutch farces written between 1538 and 1570.[49]

De Sotslach opens with a monologue by a drunken peasant carrying birds and eggs in a basket. The man politely greets the company present in the same manner as would be the case in a monologue, and is interrupted by a fool playing with his bauble. The fool refuses to believe that his wooden friend is suffering from the disease with which all fools are afflicted sooner or later, the growing of a stone behind one of the ears.[50] The peasant does not immediately recognize the other person as a fool and instead mistakes him for the Devil. The misunderstanding is less far-fetched than it seems, for all over Europe fools and devils often co-operated. In Nuremberg, for example, the *Schembart* processions included a ship of fools called "Höll" (hell). And in Florence, a similar ship containing fools and devils was taken about on 24 June 1514.[51] Out of fear the peasant in *De Sotslach* experiences incontinence and soils himself as the fool quietly continues talking to his bauble. After a little while the fool discovers the presence of the other person. The peasant, slowly approaching him, asks a number of questions about the fool's profession. Is it very honorable? And were you born like this, or did "Marotte" whisper it all into your ears? The fool gives the impression of not needing to care about food: his dwellings are covered in pancakes and sausages, which hang at every corner of the walls, he says. His father has hundreds of children, growing up in thousands of places all over the world. Since the peasant feels very much bossed about by his wife Great Unmercifulness ("grote ongenadicheijt"), he would like to learn the art of folly so that he might be able to hold his own with her. The fool asks no more than a pound in return for his service, whereupon the peasant eagerly pays up and receives a fig named Foolish Sensation ("sot gevoelen"). This, of course, is only the beginning of the peasant's inauguration into the company of fools. Now that he has found a gullible victim for his pranks, the fool puts his bauble aside: "Nu marot ghij most hijer ruijmen tperck" ("Well, marot, you will have to clear the way"). He pours a jug of beer over the peasant's head, besmirches his face, and, in a gesture worthy of a magician, pulls an egg out of his nose. Feeling completely rejuvenated, the peasant now wants to have his own cap and bells. Warning him not to spread any bad smells, the fool promises the man that he will teach him a genuine fools' egg-dance. Once he has blown into a horn filled with soot, the peasant has now, according to the fool, earned his own cap. He will obtain it in the town of "bothuijsen" ("Obtuse-borough") only a mile away from the land of Cockaigne at the other side of the sea. Two boats will sail there, the skippers of which answer to the names of Poverty and Poor. There the local bishop will grant him his much desired promotion.

VII

In his exhibition catalogue *Beeld van de andere, vertoog over het zelf*, Paul Vandenbroeck explains the fool's great popularity at the turn of the sixteenth century as being caused by the fact that a direct relationship is gradually being established between folly and vice on the one hand and reason and virtue on the other. In other words, whatever is reasonable is good, whereas folly results in evil. During the high Middle Ages the argument would have been made precisely in the opposite direction: virtue leads to knowledge and wisdom, vice to folly. According to Vandenbroeck, the increasing stress on reason automatically makes folly a central concept for discussion.[52] It is especially in the works of Sebastian Brant and Desiderius Erasmus that this new attitude towards folly is found. Whoever has himself been tempted by the rich, seductive, morally corrupt world will display the characteristics of a fool and is liable to be driven off in a Ship of Fools—or, as in one example noted above, in Charon's boat.

In the Dutch rhetoricians' drama, however, fools act in quite a different way. They serve the function of showing how to avoid being carried away in ships of fools, for they, or their baubles, explicitly warn people by ridiculing foolish behavior. This is, for example, the central message of *Van Nyeuvont, Loosheit ende Practike*. Implicitly, the same advice is also given in *Den Eedt van Meester Oom*: people from various trades and professions will be included in the empire of folly that Oomken intends to establish shortly. Whether the audience witnessing the event will regard this invitation as an honor is highly questionable. The Haarlem monologue *Een Marot noodt ter Bruijloft* would seem to have been designed to tempt very few in the audience to travel to Flanders to attend the wedding of "Dwaeseg die

Grijffijn" and the Duke of Mal. The fools in the *Tafelspel van Drie Sotten* in the end change their costumes and decide to alter their way of life by henceforth acting more wisely. Halff Verdoelt, the fool in *Bruer Willeken*, eventually decides to withdraw from the world and return to his monastery. Finally, it is in fact the peasant in *De Sotslach* who should actually be regarded as the greatest fool. Reviewing these and other texts will lead to one very simple conclusion: fools in Dutch rhetoricians' drama are ultimately not foolish at all.

NOTES

[1] Throughout the present article the term 'Dutch' is used for the language and the culture of both the northern (mainly Holland and Zeeland) and the southern Low Countries (mainly Flanders and Brabant). J. J. Mak, *De rederijkers* (Amsterdam: P. N. van Kampen, 1944), pp. 11–12, briefly discusses the influence of the fool guilds on the origin of the Chambers of Rhetoric.

[2] See Herman Pleij, "Van keikoppen en droge jonkers: Spotgezelschappen, wijkverenigingen en het jongerengericht in de literatuur en het culturele leven van de late middeleeuwen," *Volkskundig Bulletin*, 15 (1989), 297–315, who argues that a dozen or more Chambers of Rhetoric evolved from youth companies. He refers to one example in which the records attest to the transformation, in 1454–55, of a youth association into a Chamber of Rhetoric: Dendermonde's "Leewercke" ("The Lark").

[3] For a discussion of the connection between French *Puys* and Flemish Chambers of Rhetoric, see Eug. de Bock, *Opstellen over Colijn van Rijssele en andere rederijkers* (Antwerp: De Sikkel, 1958), pp. 5–16.

[4] Dirk Coigneau *et al.*, *Uyt Ionsten Versaemt: Het Landjuweel van 1561 te Antwerpen* (Brussels: Koninklijke Bibliotheek Albert I, 1994), p. 29.

[5] Paul Vandenbroeck, *Beeld van de andere, vertoog over het zelf: Over wilden en narren, boeren en bedelaars* (Antwerp: Koninklijk Museum voor Schone Kunsten, 1987), p. 41.

[6] Dirc Potter, *Blome der Doechden*, in *Dat Bouck der Bloemen*, ed. Fr. P. Stephanus Schoutens (Hoogstraten: L. Van Hoof-Roelans, 1904), p. 44, as quoted by H. Pleij, "De zot als maatschappelijk houvast in de overgang van middeleeuwen naar moderne tijd," *Groniek: Historisch tijdschrift*, 109 (1990), 19–39.

[7] A. V[iaene], "Zotten en innocenten van der stede," *Biekorf*, 40 (1934), 47–50.

[8] For the social position of fools at the end of the Middle Ages, see Vandenbroeck, *Beeld van de andere, vertoog over het zelf*, pp. 40–61.

[9] *Spel van den Somer ende van den Winter*, in *Middelnederlandsche Dramatische Poëzie*, ed. P. Leendertz, Jr. (Leiden: A. W. Sijthoff, 1907), pp. 436–41.

[10] Jeanette M. Hollaar and E. W. F. van den Elzen, "Het vroegste toneelleven in enkele Noordnederlandse plaatsen," *Nieuwe Taalgids*, 73 (1980), 311–12. For the German *Sankt Pauler Neidhartspiel*, see *Neidhartspiele*, ed. John Margett (Graz: Akademische Druck- u. Verlagsanstalt, 1982), pp. 11–16, 276–83.

[11] Jeanette M. Hollaar and E. W. F. van den Elzen, "Toneelleven in Deventer in de vijftiende en zestiende eeuw," *Nieuwe Taalgids*, 73 (1980), 413.

[12] *Van Nyeuvont, Loosheit ende Practike: Hoe sij Vrou Lortse verheffen*, ed. E. Neurdenburg (Utrecht: A. Oosthoek, 1910).

[13] L. van Puyvelde, "Het Ontstaan van het Modern Tooneel in de Oude Nederlanden: De Oudste Vermeldingen in de Rekeningen," *Verslagen en Mededeelingen van de Koninklijke Vlaamsche Academie* (1922), p. 937. The story also appeared in one of the French *Miracles de Nostre Dame*. We do not know, of course, whether the Dutch play was adapted from a narrative source or from this French dramatic version.

[14] Van Puyvelde, "Het Ontstaan van het Modern Tooneel in de Oude Nederlanden," p. 940.

[15] *Van Nyeuvont, Loosheit ende Practike*, ed. Neurdenburg, p. 68 (ll. 136–40).

[16] Ibid., p. 83 (ll. 468–69).

[17] Ibid., p. 71 (ll. 167–76).

[18] Ibid., p. 76 (ll. 308–09).

[19] *Trou Moet Blijcken: bronnenuitgave van de boeken der Haarlemse rederijkerskamer 'de Pellicanisten'*, ed. W. N. M. Hüsken, B. A. M. Ramakers, and F. A. M. Schaars (Assen: Uitgeverij Quarto, 1994), IV, fols. 29^r-35^r.

[20] *Cort verhael van tprincipael in Leyden bedreven by sotten meest die op Vrou Lors feest waren verschreven* (Leyden: Jan Claesz. van Dorp, 1596). See also Anneke Huisman and Johan Koppenol, *Daer compt de Lotery met trommels en trompetten! Loterijen in de Nederlanden tot 1726* (Hilversum: Verloren, 1991), pp. 56–61.

[21] E. van Autenboer, *Volksfeesten en rederijkers te Mechelen (1400–1600)* (Ghent: Koninklijke Vlaamse Academie voor Taal- en Letterkunde, 1962), pp. 45, 72.

[22] For this chronicle see W. van Eeghem, "Rhetores Bruxellenses, XVI: Jan Colyns alias Walravens," *Revue belge de philologie et d'histoire*, 15 (1936), 74–78.

[23] The text of this "decree" has been edited by Herman Pleij; see his *Het gilde van de Blauwe Schuit: Literatuur, volksfeest en burgermoraal in de late middeleeuwen* (Amsterdam: Meulenhoff, 1979), pp. 248–52. For further information concerning the festival, see the same author's "Volksfeest en toneel in de middeleeuwen, I: De zot draait de rollen om," *De Revisor*, 3 (1976), 52–63.

[24] Pleij, *Het gilde*, p. 248.

[25] *Een ander tafelspel*, in the collection "Trou Moet Blijcken," Book I, fols. 97ᵛ–102ʳ; in *Trou Moet Blijcken*, ed. Hüsken, Ramakers, and Schaars (Assen: Uitgeverij Quarto, forthcoming), Vol. VIII.

[26] The dinner plays may be divided into "tafelspelen in enge zin" ("dinner plays in a narrow sense," meant for a specific occasion) and "tafelspelen in ruimere zin" ("dinner plays in a broader sense," in which the occasion was left open so that, at a client's request, the basic text could be altered according to the occasion). See Wim Hüsken, "De gelegenheidsdichter Cornelis Everaert en zijn tafelspelen in enge en ruimere zin," *Verslagen en mededelingen van de Koninklijke Academie voor Nederlandse taal- en letterkunde* (1992), pp. 62–78.

[27] *Een Marot noodt ter Bruijloft*, in *Het Nederlandsche Kluchtspel van de 14e tot de 18e eeuw*, ed. J. van Vloten, 2nd ed. (Haarlem: W. C. de Graaf, 1877), I, 187–90.

[28] *Een Tafelspel van Meester Kackadoris ende een Doof wijf met Ayeren* (Amsterdam: Ewout Muller, 1596), sigs. B5ᵛ–B6ᵛ.

[29] Ibid., sig. B6ʳ–B6ᵛ.

[30] *Drie schandaleuse spelen (Brussel 1559)*, ed. Willem van Eeghem (Antwerp: De Sikkel, 1937), p. 30.

[31] The term *mues* may also refer instead to bagpipes. Later in the play (ibid., p. 32), the *mues* is mentioned again: "desen mues sal bij gans herssebeck*en* || met zijnen tanden ewe*n* nese af trecken || siten grijsen al waer hij va*n* ho*n*ger flau" ("This mouse will, by God's skull, pull off your nose with its teeth. See how it opens its mouth wide as if faint with hunger").

[32] Ibid., p. 51.

[33] Ibid., p. 57.

[34] Ibid., p. 61.

[35] This story was also dramatized in a French drama; see *Farce nouvelle de trois Amoureux de la Croix*, in *Recueil de farces françaises inédites du XVᵉ siècle*, ed. Gustave Cohen (Cambridge: Medieval Academy of America, 1949), pp. 57–66. For other versions in prose, see, for example, *Een Nyeuwe Clucht Boeck*, ed. Herman Pleij *et al.* (Muiderberg: Dick Coutinho, 1983), pp. 132–34.

[36] These plays were performed in 1591 in Amsterdam and were printed in the same year by Herman Jansz. Muller. The prologue discussed here belongs to the fifth play, on liberating prisoners: *T'vijfste Spel, van die Wercken der Bermherticheyt*, sigs. K6ᵛ–K8ᵛ.

[37] W. L. de Vreese, "Een spel van Charon de helsche schippere," *Nederlandsche Dicht- en Kunsthalle*, 17 (1895), 261–313.

[38] For Lucian's "Charon, or the Inspectors," see *Lucian*, ed. A. M. Harmon, Loeb Classical Library (1915; rpt. London: William Heinemann, 1960), II, 395–447.

[39] De Vreese, "Een spel van Charon," p. 289 (l. 307).

[40] Ibid., p. 279 (l. 19).

[41] Ibid., p. 281 (ll. 71–74).

[42] Ibid., p. 287 (ll. 245–47).

[43] J. F. Vanderheyden, *Het thema en de uitbeelding van den dood in de poëzie der late Middeleeuwen en der vroege Renaissance in de Nederlanden* (Ghent: Koninklijke Vlaamsche Academie, 1930), pp. 239–40.

[44] *Bruer Willeken*, in *De Roode Roos: Zinnespelen en andere tooneelstukken der zestiende eeuw*, ed. Osc. van den Daele and Fr. van Veerdeghem (Bergen: Dequesne-Masquillier en Zonen, 1899), p. 216.

[45] For information about events in 1565 and an edition of the Haarlem play, see Lauris Jansz., *Een spel van sinnen beroerende Het Cooren*, ed. W. M. H. Hummelen and G. R. W. Dibbets (Zutphen: W. J. Thieme, 1985).

[46] *Spelen van Cornelis Everaert*, ed. J. W. Muller and L. Scharpé (Leiden: E. J. Brill, 1899–1920), pp. 421–35, 632–35.

[47] *Minckijsers*, in *Trou Moet Blijcken*, ed. Hüsken, Ramakers, and Schaars (Assen: Uitgeverij Quarto, 1992), I, fols. 106^{v}–121^{v}.

[48] Lambrecht Dirrixsz. de Vult, *Tafelspel van Jonstige Minne en Boerdelick Wesen*, in J. van Vloten, ed., "Drie tafelspelen," *De Dietsche Warande*, 10 (1874), 116–31.

[49] *De Sotslach: Klucht uit ca. 1550*, ed. Frederik Lyna and Willem van Eeghem (Brussels: De Vrienden van het Boek, 1932). The title of this play is supplied by the editors; it is explicitly meant to allude to the word "ridderslag" ("knight's accolade").

[50] See especially the example by Hieronymus Bosch (*The Extraction of the Stone of Madness*) in the Museo del Prado in Madrid.

[51] Vandenbroeck, *Beeld van de andere*, pp. 41–42.

[52] Ibid., p. 40.

Sienese Fools, Comic Captains, and Every Fop in His Humor

Robert W. Leslie

It would seem self-evident that satirists' targets are the evils of their times and therefore that the characters which embody those evils should also result from suggestions in the *tempora* and *mores* of the author's own milieu. Such a view, however, is not wholly valid. Writers working within a literary tradition have always tended to adopt the *topoi* and typology of that tradition as required and, rather than invent a type wholesale from topical sources, have often contributed to the development of an existing characterization by adapting it to present need. The highly imitative nature of Renaissance culture and its relative lack of concern for what modern readers have come to regard as the importance of originality tended to promote this slow developmental mode of creation. In this paper I shall examine just such a development and, in so doing, trace a literary line which extends from an early Italian burlesque, the Sienese Fool, to the foppish inhabitants of Ben Jonson's "humors" plays and beyond. As such, the present study is an attempt at a comparative study that will focus on a type of the fool in drama that is a distinctive development of the post-medieval period.

The Sienese fool, unlike the wily *zanni* or the more saturnalian manifestations of the court fool, displays no wit or wisdom. He is a simple model of triviality and foolishness—qualities traditionally ascribed to the Sienese in Northern Italian literature dating back at least as far as Dante's *Inferno*. In Canto XXIX the false magician Griffolino of Arezzo derides the "senno poco" ("little sense" [l. 114]) of his one-time dupe Albero of Siena, while Dante's subsequent comment to Virgil "Or fu già mai/ gente sí vana come la sanese?" ("Now were there ever people as fatuous as the Sienese?" [ll. 121–22])[1] reveals the more generally contemptuous attitude felt towards their southern neighbor by the austere Florentines, who were constrained by sumptuary laws and the hard-working ethos of bourgeois morality. John D. Sinclair notes the attraction of Sienese society for magical frauds such as Griffolino and the alchemist Capocchio:

> It was such a wealthy, wanton and frivolous society as that of Siena, and especially such a group in it as the Spendthrift Club, that offered the most fruitful field of operations for these "apes of nature". The studied elegance and aristocratic refinement of the life, as of the art, of thirteenth and fourteenth century Siena was apt to be despised by the more robust and bourgeois spirit of Florence and Dante does not miss his chance here or elsewhere.[2]

Boccaccio likewise, in *Decameron* VII.3 and VII.10, shows scant respect for the Sienese and indicates the ease with which they may be cuckolded, while in VII.10 he derides their "besciaggine" ("foolishness").[3] That these are not isolated or atypical instances is confirmed by Angela Casella, who lists a dozen cases in which the Sienese fool is made the butt of satirically-minded poets.[4] In one example, the chivalric romance *Morgante* by Luigi Pulci (1432–84), the hero Rinaldo is presented with a pavilion the walls of which are decorated with representations of the four elements. That which depicts the creatures of the air provides the excuse for an authorial aside recalling an embarrassing purchase made by a Sienese:

> Il picchio v'era e va volando a scosse,
> che'l comperò tre lire, è poco, un besso;
> perchè e' pensò ch'un pappagallo fosse,
> mandollo a Corsignan, poi non fu desso,
> tanto che Siena ha ancor le gote rosse.[5]
>
> (The woodpecker there that flew swift back and forth
> for a song by a Sienese fool was late bought

> who firmly deceiv'd 'twas a parrot in truth,
> sent the bird to Pope Pius who said it was not,
> so that Sienese faces are still red and hot.)[6]

And the type could still provide amusement for the *novellieri* of the early cinquecento, as the *giornata prima* of Firenzuola's *Ragionamenti* (1525) confirms:

> L'anno del Giubileo andava a Roma alla perdonanza una mona Selvaggia di Neri Foraboschi, e fra gli altri che l'aveva con lei, era un suo famiglio che era in su 'n un caval vetturino, il quale oltre agli altri difetti era cieco da un occhio. Or passando costor per Siena, quando e' furon vicini alle case di quei Piccoluomini, un giovanetto de la terra, che era in sull'uscio, veggendolo, disse ad un che gli era da canto: «Mira, quel cavallo è fiorentino». La Selvaggia udendo costui così parlare gli domandò della cagione; a cui egli senza pensar più oltre rispose: «Perciocché gli era cieco». A cui la donna, come a chi parve esser trafitta sul vivo, disse: «Giovane, tu erri, imperocché questo cavallo è sanese, nè puote per modo alcuno essere fiorentino». «Come sanese?»—rispose il giovane, ridendo come se di lei si facesse beffe—e perché?». Ed ella: «Perciocché egli è una bestia».[7]

> (In the year of the Jubilee, a certain Mistress Selvaggia, of the house of Neri Foraboschi, was traveling to Rome for the Absolution. She had in her entourage a man-servant who rode a draft-horse which, amongst its other defects, was blind in one eye. Now as they were passing through Siena and nearing the houses of the Piccoluomini family, a local lad standing in a doorway saw them and remarked to the person next to him: "Look, that horse is from Florence." Selvaggia, hearing him speak thus, asked him to explain, and, without a moment's thought, he replied: "Because it's blind." At this the lady, mortally offended, said: "Young man, you are mistaken, for, since this horse is Sienese, there is no way in which it could be from Florence." "Sienese?" responded the lad, laughing as though to mock her. "Why do you say that?" "Because," she replied, "he is a dumb brute.")

Dramatic poets were also to employ the *topos*, the first example in the vernacular being that of the "Sanese" in Ariosto's *Suppositi* (prose version 1509; Englished by

George Gascoigne, in 1566, as *Supposes*) who is gulled into impersonating Filogono, the *innamorato*'s father by being told that there is a Ducal interdict in force against citizens of Siena.[8] He is a natural fool, and his naiveté is suggested when he is described as "non essere de li più pratichi uomini del mondo" ("not being one of the most able men in the world" [II.i.149]) and confirmed by the observation that "non debbe avere troppa esperienzia" ("he can't have had much experience" [II.i.158]) while the confrontation (IV.v) between the counterfeit Filogono, timorously maintaining his role from behind a door, and the real Filogono, gradually losing his temper, provides one of the funniest scenes of the play (as well as perhaps suggesting the dialogue of the two Dromios in *The Comedy of Errors* III.i). Although the Sanese is unquestionably foolish, he is treated with some sympathy and demonstrates a tolerant and forgiving nature when all is revealed: "mi giova avere imparato, senza alcuno mio danno, di essere un'altra volta più cauto et ogni cosa non credere così al primo tratto. E tanto più, essendo stata trama amorosa, leggermente e senza un minimo sdegno me ne passo" ("I'm glad that, without any harm to my person, I have learned to be more careful in the future and not to take everything at face value. Furthermore, since this was occasioned by love, I shall overlook it cheerfully and without the slightest quibble" [V.vii. 3–8]).

The Sienese fool is treated rather more harshly in Pietro Aretino's *La cortigiana* (*The Courtly Comedy*, c.1535).[9] This play loosely combines two plots, one of which not only recalls the traditional foolishness of the Sienese but, in an important development of the type as a stock theatrical character, also cruelly mocks the "studied elegance and aristocratic refinement" that Sinclair notes. Messer Maco, a particularly gullible and stupid Sienese, has come to Rome, home of his father's old friend Parabolano, with the foolish idea of becoming a cardinal and obtaining the favor of the King of France. He falls in with a trickster, Maestro Andrea, who tells him that one must first become a courtier in order to obtain such preferment. Andrea offers his services as Maco's instructor and proceeds to gull him mercilessly. Maco is finally persuaded that a dose of purgatives and parboiling in a cauldron will magically transform him into a courtier. After undergoing this treatment, he confidently presents himself at the door of Camilla, a courtesan with whom he is infatuated, and demands entry by right as a courtier. He is beaten and chased away by "Spaniards" who are, in reality, Andrea and his cronies. He then encounters Parabolano, who restores peace and invites the cast to dinner at his house.

Maco is rehearsed in his role as courtier by his servant, Sanese:

> *San.* Dite la Signoria vostra. Non udiste il maestro, che disse: mi raccomando a la Signoria vostra?
>
> *M. Maco.* Mi raccomando a la Signoria vostra. Con la beretta in mano, è vero?
>
> *San.* Signor sì. Tiratevi la persona in le gambe, acconciatevi la veste a dosso, sputate tondo, o bene. Passeggiate largo, bene, benissimo. (I.iii; p. 92)
>
> (*San.* You say "your Lordship." Didn't you hear the maestro say "I commend myself to Your Lordship"?
>
> *M. Maco.* "I commend myself to Your Lordship." With my cap in my hand, like this?
>
> *San.* Yes, sir. Draw your body down towards your legs, tuck your gown behind you, and have a good spit—oh, well done. Now stroll briskly off—good, very good.)

And Maestro Andrea lists the traits of a courtier: "La principal cosa il Cortigiano vuol saper bestemmiare, vuole esser giucatore, invidioso, puttaniere, eretico, adulatore, maldicente, sconoscente, ignorante, asino, vuol saper frappare, far la ninfa et essere agente e paziente. . . . Moglie e marito vuol dire" ("First the Courtier will know how to curse, he'll be a gambler, envious, a frequenter of whores, a heretic, a flatterer, a scandal-monger, and an ungrateful ignorant ass. He'll know how to boast, play the popinjay, and take both the active and the passive role. . . . Meaning the husband's and the wife's" [I.xxii; pp. 100–01]). Aretino's satirical reference to homosexuality at the Roman court is continued when Maestro Andrea promises the foolish Maco (I.xxii; p. 101) that, in his second lesson in how to be a courtier, "tratteremo del Culiseo . . . Il tesoro e la consolazion di Roma" ("we'll talk about the Col-ass-eum . . . the treasure and consolation of Rome"). Andrea also recommends (I.xxii; p. 101) that the aspiring Courtier always carry a copy of "Petrarchino" ("good old Petrarch") to impress. Maco takes this a step further and pens some appalling doggerel to his courtesan:

> O stelluza d'amore, o angel d'orto,
> Faccia di legno e viso d'oriente,
> Io sto più mal di voi la nave in porto.
> Dormo la notte a la tempesta e al vento:
> Le tue belleze vennero di Francia,
> Come che Giuda che si strangoloe,
> Per amor tuo mi fo Cortigiano io
> Non aspetto già mai cotal desio. (II.xii; p. 113)
>
> (Love's star, of the cabbage patch you are the angel
> Your face carved like wood in an eastern visage.
> Tho' my ship's in port I'm increasingly unwell
> O'er you; through my night's sleep the storm and wind rage.
> Your beautiful features in France had their birthing,
> Just as did old Judas who choked himself dead.
> I expect I shall never desire such an ending,
> Through love of you I'll be a Courtier instead.)

The "Courtier" he becomes has a somewhat rough and soldierly disposition: "Vo' bestemmiare, vo' portar l'arme,/ vo' chiavellare tutte tutte le Signore" ("I'll curse, carry arms, and tup all, yes all, the Ladies" [IV.xviii; p. 149]). And Andrea reports that, after his transformation, Maco's protestations of love to Camilla have taken on a truly cosmopolitan air: "frappa a la napolitana, sospira a la spagnarda, ride a la sanese, e prega a la cortigiana, e la vuol copulare a tutte le fogge del mondo" ("he boasts in the manner of a Neapolitan, sighs in the style of a Spaniard, laughs like a Sienese, implores like a Courtier, and wants to copulate with her in every way known to the world" [V.v; p. 154]). Maco's military manner, Neapolitan boasting, and Spanish sighs are an early sign of the confluence of the Sienese fool with the captain that is the foolish and boastful warrior of the Italian stage.

The captain, inspired ultimately by the reappearance of the *miles gloriosus* in the neo-classical drama, became a stock character in the *commedia dell'arte*. Through constant improvisation, there developed those characteristics which were to define the type: self-aggrandizement, amorousness, exaggerated courtesies, cowardice, and frequently Spanish or Neapolitan nationality since Naples, with its Spanish ruling house, was sometimes diplomatically substituted for Spain. He was generally furnished with a manservant whose appetite for food usually equalled the captain's desire for fame and who harbored few illusions about his master's prowess.

Of the unmasked characters *dell'arte*, the captain is perhaps the most verbally impressive. A number of compilations of his boasting speeches survive, most famously that of Francesco Andreini of the Gelosi company: *Le bravure del Capitano Spavento* (*The Deeds of Captain Fear*), published in 1608. Andreini's character claims to have trounced the Olympian gods (Dialogue 2), and he vaunts not only his military exploits but also his amatory abilities as he declares that he has made love to Death herself (Dialogue 7) —and thus that he thereby fathered the Guelf and Ghibelline factions.[10]

The captain was generally the butt of jokes about his cowardice, and his frequent portrayal as an over-punctilious, amorous, but threadbare Spaniard milked the obvious potential in exploiting audience resentment against an occupying power. He could also, on occasion, play the role of the Lover, albeit a somewhat comical one, and some of the *innamorato*'s characteristics seem to have been shared with him. It is perhaps indicative of this that Andreini himself started as the lover but crossed over to the captain's part: "mi compiacqui di rappresentar nelle Comedie la parte del Milite superbo, ambitioso, e vantatore, facendomi chiamare il Capitan Spauento da Vall'Inferna. E talmente mi compiacqui in essa, ch'io lasciai di recitare la parte mia principale, la quale era quella dell'innamorato" ("I amused myself in the Comedies by playing the part of the proud, ambitious, and boastful Warrior under the name of Captain Fear of Hell Valley. In fact it amused me so much that I left off playing my principal role which was that of the lover").[11]

A character in Antonfrancesco Grazzini's *La strega* (*The Witch,* c.1547) perfectly combines the foolishness and frivolity of the Sienese fool with the martial aspirations and boasting of the captain.[12] Like *La cortigiana, La strega* has a double plot whose themes are, however, somewhat more closely intertwined than those of Aretino's play. Defying her husband and other lovers, Fabrizio succeeds in winning Bia and keeps her hidden in the house of an old witch called Mona Sabatina. Seeking shelter in the same house is his friend Orazio, son of Luc'Antonio Palermini, who has returned secretly to Florence with a noble young Genoese lady, Violante. To avoid compromising Violante, he does not wish to be recognized and is in disguise. His father believes he has been captured by the Turks and put to death. The two couples live happily enough until money begins to run short. Orazio realizes that he must get money from his father, and, in order to obtain it more readily, they agree that his arrival will be announced by Fabrizio as if he had learned of his coming through Sabatina's prophetic witchery.

A rich but foolish orphan called Taddeo Saliscendi has fallen in love with Geva, the sister of Orazio, but Luc'Antonio refuses to accept him since she is now his heir and he wishes to make a more socially advantageous match for her. A despairing Taddeo, ill-advised by his servant Farfanicchio, believes that a military reputation might win Geva and decides to join the army. His mother, Bartolommea, and his uncle Bonifazio, after failing to dissuade him, have recourse to Sabatina.

Violante's mother, Mona Oretta, arriving in Florence with her servant Clemenza, is searching for her daughter. She meets her returning from Mass, but Violante, fearful of losing her Orazio, avoids her and hurriedly withdraws into Sabatina's house. Luc'Antonio is passing by and recognizes M. Oretta as the widow of Miraboni, his one-time host in Genoa. He takes her to his home and promises to help her. When Orazio appears, as predicted by Fabrizio, all is explained, and the play ends with Orazio marrying Violante and Taddeo marrying Geva.

Taddeo, although Florentine, is clearly cast in the mould of the Sienese fool. Like Maco, he is a poetaster, and his verses (sung to the accompaniment of the harp), while not as exaggeratedly clumsy as those of Maco, are a clichéd mixture of paradoxical conceit, metaphoric allusion, and self-vaunting classicism:

> La Geva mia adesso è bianca e bruna,
> bruna la veste, ma bianca la carne;
> l'è più brillante che non è la luna;
> e più frullante che non son le starne.
> Bisogna essere amico di Fortuna,
> di Venere e d'Amor, chi vuol beccarne,
> come son io, amante e semideo:
> viva la Geva e 'l suo sposo Taddeo. (V.viii; p. 105)
>
> (Now Geva, who's mine, is at once dark and fair,
> for her flesh shows so fair 'gainst the dark of her gown.
> More lively than partridges beating the air,
> so is she, and her brilliance surpasses the moon.
> Whoever would win her must first be an ally
> of Fortune, and Venus and Cupid her son,
> a lover who's semi-divine, just as am I.
> Long life to us! Geva's by Taddeo won.)

Grazzini adds an original element to the traditional typology of the Sienese fool by his portrayal of Taddeo as a *nouveau riche*: "l'avol suo fu carbonaio, e il padre mulattiere" ("his grandfather was a coalman, and his father a mule-driver" [I.ii; p. 63]). Despite these humble if well-heeled origins, Taddeo requires his servant to address him as "signore" ("My Lord"), especially in public: "Sì, dammi ora di signore; dove egli importava e tra la gente, non te ne ricordasti tu mai" ("Yes, now you address me as My Lord; where it mattered, when people were around, you never remembered" [III.i; p. 73]). His wish to marry Geva is indicative of *borghese* ambitions to earn respectability by marrying into the gentry, but Taddeo's clumsy attempts to ape his social superiors are comically subverted as, trying to keep abreast of fashion, he turns himself into a visual laughing-stock. Two editions of the play appeared in Venice in 1582, the first in duodecimo, the second in octavo. In the duodecimo version, additional comments on the setting and characters appear after the listing of the *Dramatis Personae.*[13] Among them is one which underlines Taddeo's sartorial changeability: "Avvertiscasi che Taddeo esce fuori sempre vestito variamente, come leggendo mostra la comedia." (Taddeo is always dressed differently when he comes onstage, as a reading of the comedy shows [Notes, p. 110]).

Farfanicchio's listing of the various national origins of Taddeo's clothing and personality recalls the international patchwork of character exhibited by Maco in *La cortigiana*: "Voi avete, cioè la signoria vostra, ha la berretta alla tedesca, la cappa alla franzese, il saione alla fiorentina, il colletto sòpravi alla spagnuola, le calze alla guascona, le scarpette alla romanesca, il viso alla fiesolana, il cervello alla sanese, e lo spennacchio alla giannetta" ("You have—I mean Your Lordship has—a German cap, a French cloak, a Florentine doublet, and, above it, a Spanish collar; Gascon hose, Roman slippers, a Fiesolan face but a Sienese brain, and the plumes of an Andalusian pony" [III.i; pp. 73–74]). The reference to Taddeo's "Sienese brain," coupled with his generally foolish demeanor, confirms the character within the tradition of the Sienese fool. The role is, however, given added complexity and interest by an admixture of traits deriving from the captain.

The captain frequently boasted of divine ancestry or capability—e.g., *Gli duoi fratelli rivali* (*The Two Rival Brothers*) of c.1595 by Giambattista Della Porta in which Captain Martebellonio claims to derive his name from his war-god parents, Mars and Bellona, and, as we have seen, Andreini's Capitano Spavento lauds himself as more than a match for Olympus. The penultimate line of Taddeo's song to Geva defines him as a demigod—a statement which has no dramatic function or basis except to assert the character's debt to the typology of the captain. When Taddeo is trying on his armor he boasts: "Oh, io son fiero! io son terribile! io me lo veggo, io lo conosco; guarti vigliacco, ahi! dico io, guarti, che l'ombra mia mi fa paura" ("Oh, I'm fierce! I'm terrible! I see it in myself and I recognize it; hey coward, beware! I say beware, for my shadow even scares me" [IV.ii, p. 81]). One of the attractions of a soldier's life to him is that he will be able to "minacciare, bravare, bestemmiare anche e dare" ("threaten, swagger, even curse and thump people" [III.i; p. 74]), and, as his uncle's maid Verdiana notes, he practices swordplay with his servant: "Giuoca di spada e di schermaglia con quel maledetto Farfanicchiuzzo" ("He's playing at fencing and skirmishing with that damn fool Farfanicchio" [V.v; p. 99]). However, his military pretensions, like those of the Captain, are nothing more than fantasy, and he is stunned when the realities of war are explained to him:

> *Bonifazio.* Alla guerra si patisce caldo, freddo, fame, sete e sonno; dormesi il più delle volte coll'arme in dosso, e sopra lo spazzo; e spesso, quando altri si vorrebbe riposare, bisogna fare alto e camminare, ire alle scaramucce o far le guardie; e se per disgrazia tu amalassi, lasciamo andare i medici e le medecine, non che altro, non puoi avere spesso dell'acqua e del pane a tua posta.
>
> *Taddeo.* Come? oh! non v'è egli del marzapane, del trebbiano, dei zuccherini e delle mele cotte? (IV.iv; pp. 85–86)
>
> (*Bonifazio.* In the wars you suffer from the heat, the cold,

> hunger, thirst, and weariness; you usually sleep with your weapons strapped on and nothing to cover you; and often, when you would far rather sleep, you have to break camp and march, go skirmishing, or stand guard. If, by some misfortune, you fall ill, forget about doctors and medicine, let alone anything else. Much of the time your post won't even have water or bread.
>
> *Taddeo*. What? Oh! Isn't there any marzipan or Trebbiano wine or sweets or baked apples there?)

After Bonifazio's descriptions, Taddeo begins to consider being a warrior on a more congenial battlefield: "La darò pel mezzo a casa le mondane e alle taverne" ("I'll wage [war] right through the whorehouses and taverns" [IV.iii; p. 86]).

Critical opinion has tended to view Taddeo as simply a variant on the *miles gloriosus* alone,[14] but this way of categorizing him ignores a number of key points. The captain, for all his foolishness, requires a certain capacity for artifice in order to survive—his boasts are generally aimed at securing him some degree of social advancement—while Taddeo is a natural fool. The captain tends to be threadbare (cf. Armado in *Love's Labor's Lost*), while Taddeo is a sartorial popinjay. And, by the same token, Taddeo is rich while the captain's famished servants testify to their master's poverty. Taddeo is as much the Sienese fool as he is the captain, and in blending these two types Grazzini has created a novel addition to the theatrical roster of stock characters. The characteristics of this new type may be identified as follows:

1. Middling social status
2. Upward social aspirations
3. Gullibility
4. Boastfulness
5. Amorous intent
6. Mediocre and/or plagiarizing poet/musician
7. Ostentation in dress—usually wearing an assort ment of foreign garments

8. Affectation of characteristics seen as soldierly: swearing, swordplay, whoring, bullying social inferiors

The subsequent wholesale translation of these traits into the typology of the English theater through Ben Jonson's "Humors" plays might suggest the term 'gull' for this new type were it not for the fact that the comedies of the Restoration period, in developing their somewhat Gallicized version of the character, have established 'fop' as the definitive term for this Italian theatrical hybrid.[15]

Claiming Matheo, Stephano, Fastidius Briske, *et al.* as deriving from Italian theatrical practice may be seen as perverse given that Jonson's city comedies are often viewed as peculiarly English in character. For example, in referring to the 1601 Quarto edition of *Every Man in his Humor* J. W. Lever sees the Italian setting and nomenclature as "a purely conventional backcloth for English characters and manners" and cites references to the Exchange, the Mermaid Tavern, and pence and shillings as evidence.[16] I suggest that these references are no more than a means of making a foreign milieu accessible to an English audience. The locations and items cited have direct Florentine counterparts. If you place the Exchange within the town so closely associated with the creation of modern financial institutions, or if you use shillings for currency, are you then establishing an apparently Florentine setting as really English, or are you merely translating *La Borsa* and *ducati*? The tavern is hardly a uniquely English institution, and given the similarities in English and Italian tavern names (for example, Ariosto's Ferrara had the *Moro*, the *Corona*, and the *Angelo*,[17] which may be compared to the traditional English Saracen's Head, Crown, and the Angel), the Mermaid could simply be renamed *La Sirena* without significantly altering the nature of the play. There can be no doubt that the substantial changes made to the play's internal reference system in the Folio revision of 1616 represent an attempt to adapt *Every Man in his*

Humor more fully to an English perception—with the much more anglicized "Italy" of *Every Man out of his Humor* representing an intermediary stage in this progression. I would affirm, however, that the Quarto is thoroughly Italianate in nature and represents a typically Jonsonian attempt to work within established theatrical tradition by largely observing the decorum, unities, and neoclassical formats revived and embellished by the Italian Renaissance. Even in the anglicizing of setting and nomenclature in the Folio, Jonson may be said to be following Italian precedent, given that Ariosto, in the 1529 revision of his comedy *La cassaria* (1508), had abandoned his original Greek location and characters for Italian analogues.

It would, of course, be foolish to deny that the critical focus Jonson brings to bear in *Every Man in his Humor* is turned on the English society of his day. My point is that his "humors," like the Exchange, the tavern, and the coins, all have their close counterparts in the Italian comedy of the cinquecento, have been suggested by that comic tradition, and have been employed as much because they are part of a theatrical orthodoxy to which Jonson subscribed as because they are analogues of English types. Despite Jonson's much-vaunted classicism, his comedies in fact draw much more directly on Italian sources than on Plautus and Terence. *The Alchemist*, *Volpone*, and *Epicoene* can all be related to Italian originals, *The Case is Altered* is an attempt at an Italianate romantic comedy, and arguably even the quintessentially English *Bartholomew Fair* borrows its crowded stage and typology from the theatrical practice of Aretino, Giordano Bruno, and the *commedia dell'arte*.

C. G. Child long ago suggested as a source for *The Alchemist* Giordano Bruno's play *Candelaio*, which contains a magician and an alchemist who offer their gulls respectively the love of a beautiful woman and the philosopher's stone.[18] R. C. Simonini, Jr., has added that the strong thematic similarities—both plays burlesque vice, alchemy, and pedantry—and the close literary friendship between Jonson and Bruno's friend John Florio make the assertion worthy of consideration.[19]

Volpone, in Daniel C. Boughner's view, owes much of its moral debate, implied and stated, to Machiavelli's *Prince* and *Discourses,* while his comedy *La mandragola* provides the basis for the sexual intrigue in Jonson's play.[20] To these influences I would add Jonson's debt to the *commedia dell'arte* which is evident in *Volpone*'s supporting cast. The similarity of the names Corbaccio and Corvino, the raven and the crow, underlines the characters' common origin in the multi-faceted Pantalone of the *commedia*: Corbaccio represents his greedy and foolish *vecchio* and Corvino his equally venal *becco* or cuckold. In Corvino's case the characterization is ironically stressed by his cry in Act II, Scene iii—"Hart! ere to morrow, I shall be new christen'd,/ And cald the PANTALONE *di Besogniosi,*/ About the towne" (ll. 7–9)—as he beats the disguised Volpone. The advocate, Voltore, draws on Doctor Graziano, the Bolognese lawyer, who, like Pantalone, is frequently shown to be an avaricious fool. Volpone himself is the greedy Pantalone writ large—a characterization underscored by his impersonation of a mountebank beneath Celia's window.

The burlesque of marriage in *Epicoene* has its roots in the reinterpretation of Plautus' *Casina* by Machiavelli in *La clizia* and, more particularly, by Aretino in *Il marescalco.* While the ultimate derivation of the disguised boy-bride can be seen in *Casina,* the presentation of the device is stylistically closer to the two best-known Italian renditions of the tale. *La clizia* is a lively update of the Plautine original, and Boughner argues that its crotchety *vecchio,* Nicomaco, may have provided Jonson with a ready model for Morose.[21] More specifically, the manner in which Morose is repeatedly provoked to the extremes of despair by the other characters closely resembles the cumulative provocation of the homosexual stablemaster in *Il marescalco* (Venice 1533; England 1588) who is also faced with an unwanted spouse finally revealed to be a boy. Both the stablemaster and Morose try to wriggle out of the marriage by professing their inability to consummate it—a scene which has no parallel in *Casina*.[22] The characterization of Morose as a miserly old man who is also an apparently impotent cuckold strongly suggests that, in addition to the sources listed above, Jonson has again drawn on Pantalone-as-*becco* to fill out the role.

While my primary concern is to establish an Italian line of descent for Jonson's foppish humors, I should point out that *Every Man in his Humor* and *Every Man out* show other signs of borrowing from Italian comic typology as well. Thorello's inflated jealousy and Deliro's besottedness yet again recall Pantalone—as does their mercantile profession; Bobadilla's posturing is that of the Spanish captain, and his name too hints at a Spanish origin (cf. Boabdil, the last Moorish king of Granada); Shift suggests the bravo—a lowlife cousin of the captain—with a touch of Aretino's Maestro Andrea in his role as instructor in the gentlemanly art of tobacco-taking; Doctor Clement's profession and ranting mannerisms are those of the *commedia dell' arte*'s Dottor Graziano; and Carlo Buffone's name alone suggests a zannesque character, while his instruction of Sogliardo in the art of being a gentleman is even more reminiscent of Maestro Andrea than is Shift with his tobacco class. With regard to *Every Man out of his Humor*, W. Bang demonstrated that two incidents—Sogliardo being passed off as a gentleman to Saviolina (V.ii) and Sordido's attempted suicide and recovery (III.vii and viii)—are taken from Castiglione's *Cortegiano* (probably from Sir Thomas Hoby's 1561 translation). Bang also cited Thomas Dekker's observations on *Poetaster* to demonstrate that Jonson's contemporaries were aware of his practice of drawing on foreign sources:

> And (but that I would not be thought a prater)
> I could tell you, he were a translator.
> I know the authors from whence he ha's stole,
> And could trace him too, but that I vnderstand
> 'hem not full and whole.[23]

Jonson's debt, both generic and specific, to Italian works having been established, it should come as no surprise that Stephano, of *Every Man in his Humor*, displays seven of the eight features that I have listed above as identifying the Sienese fool-captain type. He lacks only a specific reference to ostentatious clothing. It will be noted, however, that this characteristic is one that he would adopt if he had the means, for he woefully declares, "I haue no boots, thats the spite on it" (I.ii.27) and "I thinke, my legge would shewe well in a silke hose" (I.ii.47), while his eagerness to appropriate Giuliano's cloak (IV.ii.132–38) shows his desire for fine vestments. His social status, as the owner of "a faire liuing" (I.i.85), is middling, and his repeated citing of the word "gentleman" (I.i.39 and *passim*) in connection with himself underlines his desire to be seen as such. When Musco sells him a cheap sword as a Toledo rapier (II.i), both his gullibility and his martial pretensions are confirmed, while his threats against Prospero's Servingman (I.ii.23–24) and Musco (II.iii.157–58, 164–65), both safely absent, indicate a boastful nature. He cultivates the art of swearing—e.g., his "Horeson Scanderbag rogue" (I.ii.23), referring to the Servingman—and much admires Bobadilla's facility with an oath: "So, I had as liefe as an angell I could sweare as well as that gentleman!" (II.iii.111–12). Finally, he has a paramour, Marina, with whom he exchanges rings and banal verses (II.i.32–42).

Matheo is cut from the same cloth as Taddeo Saliscendi: he is of humble extraction, wishes to be a gentleman, aspires to the hand of a lady who outranks him socially, woos her with verse, and is the butt of others' ridicule. Cob, the waterbearer, neatly encapsulates his character:

> you should haue some now, would take him to be a gentleman at the least; alas God helpe the simple, his father's an honest man, a good fishmonger, and so forth: and now doth he creep and wriggle into acquaintance with all the braue gallants about the towne . . . and they flout him inuinciblie. He vseth euery day to a Marchants house (where I serue water) one M. *Thorel-*

> *los;* and here's the iest, he is in loue with my masters sister, and cals her mistres: and there he sits a whole afternoone sometimes, reading of these same abhominable, vile, (a poxe on them, I cannot abide them) rascally verses, *Poetrie, poetrie,* and speaking of *Enterludes,* 't will make a man burst to heare him: and the wenches, they doe so geere and tihe at him. (I.iii.57–71)

Rather than rely on his own verses, however, Matheo concords with Maestro Andrea's recommendation and plagiarizes those of another—"Petrarchino" in this case being replaced by the more easily recognized Kyd and Marlowe. Wishing to display a soldierly character, he employs Bobadilla to teach him fencing just as Taddeo makes use of Farfanicchio to practice fencing and skirmishing. Since Jonson's satirical arrows are somewhat more barbed than those of Grazzini, Taddeo's success with Geva does not prefigure a happy consummation of Matheo's love for his "mistres."

Fastidius Briske of *Every Man out of his Humor* shares Taddeo's trait of wearing a different costume in every scene in which he appears and also favors a similarly international mix of clothing—as is revealed when, among the clothing allegedly damaged in a duel, he lists a "*French* hat," an "*Italian* cut-worke band," and boots of "*Spanish* leather" (IV.vi.85, 90, 112). He is a "*Neat, spruce, affecting Courtier,*" and, like Aretino's Maco, he "*practiseth . . . how to salute*" (Character Summary, ll. 36–38). Maco's pledge to "tup all, yes all, the Ladies" finds reflection in Briske's simultaneous courting of the vapid Saviolina and of Fallace, Deliro's wife, while Briske's tuneless performance on the "violl *de Gambo*" (III.ix.88) is functionally identical to the banal verses that accompany Maco's and Taddeo's wooing. (Taddeo, let us remember, also plays an instrument.)

While his blend of devious cunning and poverty emphasizes the captain's side of Briske's dramatic ancestry, his would-be emulator, Fungoso, like Taddeo, is "a good simple youth" (IV.vi.144) of humble if relatively prosperous background who aspires to "*the Courtiers cut*" (Character Summary, ll. 74–75). Since his dramatic function principally appears to be the underscoring of Briske's foolish affectations, his characterization is somewhat sketchy. Similarly sketchy is that of his foppish uncle Sogliardo, who shows only typical foolishness and gentlemanly aspirations, while the even more ephemeral Clove and Orange have little more than cameo roles designed to show the essential pretentiousness of the type. Clove, however, adds a new element to the foppish character by abandoning the captain's military ranting—perhaps to avoid repeating the style of boasting already shown by Shift—and substituting the pseudo-scholarly variety associated with the *commedia dell'arte*'s Doctor Graziano.

Through the efforts of publishers such as John Wolfe and Richard Field, Italian books had a degree of general availability in Elizabethan England. Both of Machiavelli's comedies and four of Aretino's were published in London in 1588, and the *Aminta* and *Pastor Fido* followed in 1591, while the influence of the Italian drama on the native product was sufficient to cause Stephen Gosson's famous complaint that Italian comedies were "ransackt to furnish the Playe houses in London."[24] The credit for Jonson's Italianate typology, however, would seem to lie at the door of his "loving Father, & worthy Freind/ Mr John Florio: the ayde of his Muses."[25] The "ayde" presumably included access to his library as there can be no doubt that their friendship had a literary dimension. Allan H. Gilbert suggests that Jonson's characters' names in *Every Man out of his Humor* are culled from Florio's 1598 dictionary, *A Worlde of Wordes,* and identifies apparent borrowings in *Cynthia's Revels* from Florio's *Second Frutes* and *Giardino di Ricreatione;*[26] Simonini concurs and notes a further borrowing from *Second Frutes* in *Eastward Ho!*[27] Frances A. Yates points out that Jonson and Florio shared a patron, Lucy Russell, Countess of Bedford, and cites parallels between the *First Fruits* and *The Case is Altered* as well as between the *Second Frutes* and *Volpone.*[28] And Mario Praz identifies the Italian vocabulary of *Volpone* as having the same Lombardo-Venetian character as Florio's Italian in the *Worlde of Wordes*.[29] Jonson's credentials as a Latinist, his close friendship with the leading Italian teacher of his day, and his use of Machiavelli and Aretino as literary sources partially belie William Drummond's assertion that Jonson "neither doeth understand French nor Italiannes"[30]—an assertion that is perhaps best explained by Drummond's own linguistic perfectionism and a certain annoyance occasioned by the demands made on his hospitality by the appetites and self-opinionated nature of his house-guest. The question of Jonson's ability to glean plots, situations, and characters from Italian originals does not therefore arise. What is of importance is the availability of the particular source texts which could have supplied the basis for the foppish "humor."

As indicated above, Aretino's *Quattro commedie* had been published in England in 1588. Since this was presumably the source of Jonson's borrowings from *Il marescalco* for *Epicoene*, the probability is high that he was familiar with its companion play *La cortigiana* and thereby with Messer Maco and his courtly aspirations. It is not so easy to establish the contemporary availability of *La strega*—indeed the British Library's catalogue of Italian books printed between 1465–1600 lists only the Venetian editions of 1582.[31] If Jonson made use of *La strega*, he must have therefore used an imported edition. In the light of the strong similarities displayed by Stephano *et al.* and Taddeo Saliscendi, I suggest that this was in fact the case and that John Florio probably supplied the book.

Assuming that the friendship between Florio and Jonson predated the writing of *Every Man in his Humor*, and given the Italianate qualities already noted in that play, the Italian tutor's library seems the most likely starting-point for an examination of its sources. The source-lists for Florio's dictionaries presumably go some way towards cataloguing the contents of that library, and the presence therein of *La strega* is thus definitely established by its listing as a source for his *Queen Anna's Worlde of*

Wordes of 1611.[32] Whether Florio owned a copy of Grazzini's play before the writing of *Every Man in his Humor* is somewhat problematic since the 1598 *Worlde of Wordes*[33] does not, in fact, mention *La strega.* The 1598 list cannot, however, be taken as a complete and definitive guide to John Florio's library since V. Spampanato has shown that Florio contemporaneously possessed an unlisted copy of Giordano Bruno's *Candelaio,*[34] while the close parallels exhibited by Taddeo Saliscendi and the foppish "humors" argue strongly for the earlier presence of *La strega.* Moreover, since the comedy was published in 1582 with no subsequent reprints recorded prior to 1628,[35] the balance of probability favors the view that Florio's copy had been in his possession for some time.

A final factor tending to confirm Jonson's literary derivation of his foppish cast is the degree to which that cast does not in fact reflect the life of the gentry attendant upon the court. By 1598, Elizabeth's parsimony and dwindling revenues had sharply reduced the availability of patronage and advancement for ambitious courtiers. Greater opportunity came with the accession of James, whose extravagance and ready dispensation of titles created a new profligacy at court, as attested by a contemporary witness, Sir Dudley Carleton, at the time of the signing of the peace with Spain: "We cannot say that the King hath been behindhand in liberality, for at this one instant he hath given away more plate than Queen Elizabeth did in her whole reign."[36] Were Jonson's comedies principally a mirror of his times, one would expect the fop to have a greater presence in his later works. This is not the case. While he continues to portray the type—e.g., Sir Politic Would-Be in *Volpone*—the fop's role is diminished with respect to other characters as Jonson widens his range of satirical targets. The strong points of resemblance between the Sienese fool-captain synthesis and the similarly foolish Jonsonian foppish "humor," when taken together with the probable availability of key Italian texts, therefore imply that, as early as 1598, Jonson had met Florio and was already plundering Italian theatrical typology for characters well before *Volpone* and *Epicoene* were irrefutably to confirm his regard for Italian literary culture.

Jonson's work thus presents us not only with the introduction of a Continental type of the fool onto the English stage, but also with a character whose richness depends on the exploitation of a stock figure that differs in very specific ways from the native tradition as it had been established in the entertainments and plays of the late Middle Ages and early Tudor period in England.

NOTES

[1] Dante Alighieri, *La Divina Commedia*, ed. Giorgio Petrocchi (Turin: Einaudi, 1975). In the present article all translations are my own.

[2] John D. Sinclair, ed. and trans., *Inferno* (New York: Oxford Univ. Press, 1961), p. 367.

[3] Giovanni Boccaccio, *Il Decameron*, ed. Aldo Rossi (Bologna: Cappelli, 1977).

[4] Ludovico Ariosto, *Commedie*, ed. Angela Casella, Gabriella Ronchi, and Elena Varasi (Verona: Mondadori, 1974), p. 1046n.

[5] Luigi Pulci, *Il Morgante*, ed. George B. Weston (Bari: Laterza, 1930), vol. I (XIV.53.1–5).

[6] *Besso* (fool) was commonly used by Florentines at this time to refer insultingly to a Sienese (see Boccaccio's *besciaggine*). See Davide Puccini, ed., *Il Morgante* (Milan: Garzanti, 1989), pp. 458–59, for the identification of *Corsignan* as Corsignano, birthplace of Pope Pius II, subsequently renamed Pienza after its most famous son; the reference here is therefore by extension to the Pope himself, and the incident in question is supposed to have taken place in the fall of 1462. I am grateful to Mary Sisler of Rutgers University for drawing this gloss to my attention.

[7] Agnolo Firenzuola, *Opere*, ed. A. Seroni (Florence: Sansoni, 1971), p. 153.

[8] Ibid., pp. 195–257.

[9] Pietro Aretino, *Commedie*, ed. Eugenio Camerini (Milan: Sonzogno, 1962), pp. 85–167.

[10] Dialogues reproduced in Vito Pandolfi, *La Commedia dell'Arte* (Florence: Le Lettere, 1988) I, 359–81.

[11] Ibid., pp. 359–60.

[12] Antonfrancesco Grazzini, *La strega*, ed. Michel Plaisance (Abbeville: Université de Paris, 1976).

[13] Quoted in the notes in ibid., *passim*.

[14] See, for example, Giovanni Gentile, *Commedie di Antonfrancesco Grazzini detto il Lasca* (Pisa: T. Nistri, 1896); Robert J. Rodini, *Antonfrancesco Grazzini* (Madison: Univ. of Wisconsin Press, 1970); and Guido Davico Bonino, "La scrittura oggetuale del Lasca," in *Lo scrittore, il potere, la maschera* (Padua: Liviana, 1979), pp. 13–37.

[15] Citations of Jonson's plays in the present article are to the edition of C. H. Herford and Percy Simpson (1927–52; rpt. Oxford: Clarendon Press, 1954), esp. vols. III, V.

[16] Ben Jonson, *Every Man in his Humour*, ed. J. W. Lever (London: Edward Arnold, 1972), p. xxi.

[17] Ariosto, *Commedie*, p. xliv.

[18] C. G. Child, "A Source of the *Alchemist*," *The Nation*, 79 (28 July 1904), p. 75, as cited by Mario Praz, "L'Italia di Ben Jonson," in *Machiavelli in Inghilterra* (Florence: Sansoni, 1962), p. 202.

[19] R. C. Simonini, Jr., *Italian Scholarship in Renaissance England* (Chapel Hill: Univ. of North Carolina Press, 1952), p. 109.

[20] Daniel C. Boughner, *The Devil's Disciple* (Westport: Greenwood Press, 1968), pp. 113–37.

[21] Daniel C. Boughner, "Clizia and Epicoene," *Philological Quarterly*, 19 (1940), 89–91.

[22] See Oscar James Campbell, "The Relation of *Epicoene* to Aretino's *Il marescalco*," *PMLA*, 46 (1931), 752–62.

[23] In Ben Jonson, *Works* (London, 1616), p. 341, as quoted by W. Bang, "Ben Jonson und Castiglione's Cortegiano," *Englische Studien*, 36 (1906) 330–32.

[24] Stephen Gosson, *Plays Confuted in Five Actions* (London, 1582), sig. D6[v], as quoted by Louise George Clubb, *Italian Drama in Shakespeare's Time* (London: Yale Univ. Press, 1989), p. 49.

[25] Jonson's handwritten dedication to a copy of *Volpone* in the British Library, as quoted by Praz, "L'Italia di Ben Jonson," p. 203.

[26] Allan H. Gilbert, "The Italian Names in *Every Man out of his Humour*," *Studies in Philology*, 44 (1947), 195–208.

[27] R. C. Simonini, Jr., "Ben Jonson and John Florio," *Notes and Queries*, 199 (1950), 512–13.

[28] Frances A. Yates, *John Florio* (Cambridge: Cambridge Univ. Press, 1934), pp. 191, 277–81.

[29] Praz, "L'Italia di Ben Jonson," pp. 205–07.

[30] *Ben Jonson's Conversations with Drummond of Hawthornden*, ed. R. F. Patterson (Glasgow: Blackie and Son, 1924) p. 8.

[31] A. F. Johnson, V. Scholderer, and D. A. Clarke, *Short-Title Catalogue of Books Printed in Italy and of Italian Books Printed in Other Countries from 1465–1600* (London: Trustees of the British Museum, 1958).

[32] John Florio, *Queen Anne's Worlde of Wordes* (London, 1611).

[33] John Florio, *A Worlde of Wordes* (London, 1598).

[34] V. Spampanato, "Giovanni Florio: Un amico del Bruno in Inghilterra," *La Critica*, 22 (1924), 120, as quoted in Yates, *John Florio*, p. 111.

[35] The publishing history of Grazzini's works (see Rodini, *Antonfrancesco Grazzini*, pp. 178–79) shows no intervening reprints between the 1582 and 1628 editions, while *The Catalogue of 17th Century Italian Books in the British Library* (London: British Library, 1986) lists only the 1628 edition.

[36] Frederick C. Dietz, *English Public Finance 1558–1641* (New York and London: Century, 1932), p. 101, as quoted in J. P. Kenyon, *The Stuarts* (London: B. T. Batsford, 1958), p. 48.

Index

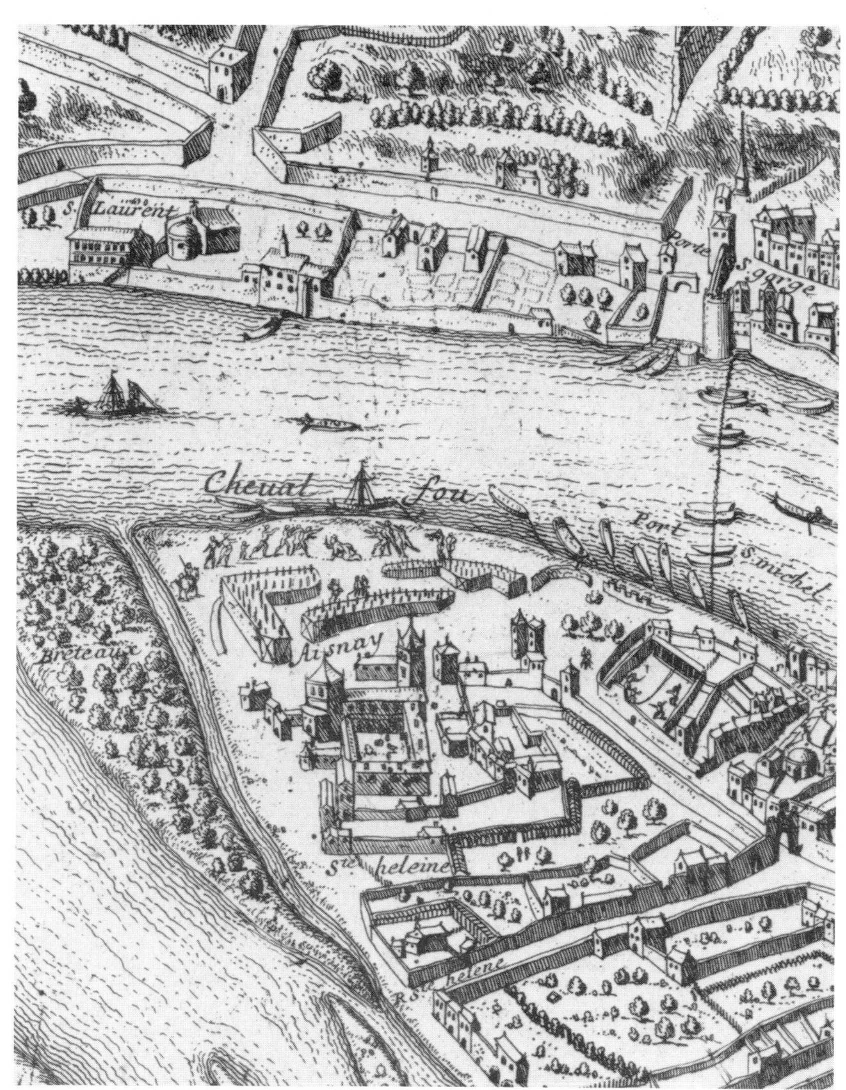

1. Detail from a map of Lyon showing the Pentecost custom of the Cheval Fol as it was perceived in the 1690's; a group berates a man on all fours, while a horseman watches. By permission of the British Library.

112 ANDREAE ALCIATI

In adulari neſcientem.

Scire cupis dominos toties cur Theſſalis ora
Mutet, & ut uarios quærat habere duces:
Neſcit adulari cuiquámue obtrudere palpum,
Regia quem morem principis omnis habet.
Sed ueluti ingenuus ſonipes, dorſo excutit omnem,
Qui moderari ipſum neſciat Hippocomen.
Nec ſæuire tamen domino fas, ultio ſola eſt,
Dura ferum ut iubeat ferre lupata magis.

2. The spirited horse, controlled by an able rider. Andrea Alciati, *Emblematvm Libellvs* (Paris: Wechsel-Jollat, 1535), p. 112. Stirling Maxwell Collection, No. 21; by permission of the Glasgow University Library, Department of Special Collections.

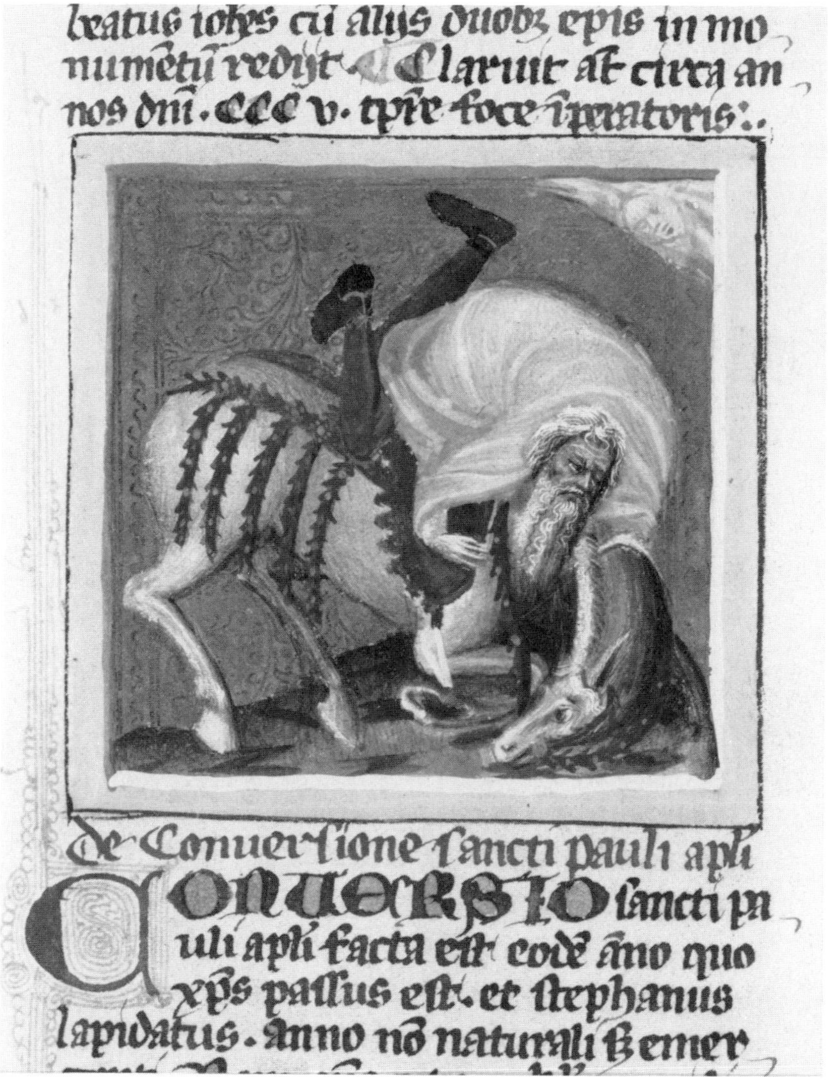

beatus iohes cu aliis duob; epis in mo
numetu redyt. Claruit aut circa an
nos dni. ccc v. tpre foce iperatoris..

de Conuersione sancti pauli apli

CONUERSIO sancti pa
uli apli facta est eod anno quo
xps passus est. et stephanus
lapidatus. Anno no naturali s emer

3. The Conversion of St. Paul, in Jacobus de Voragine, *Legenda Aurea* (Flanders, c.1405), MS. Gen. 1,111, fol. 47[r]. By permission of the Glasgow University Library, Department of Special Collections.

4. Illustration of Lechery under the text "omnem uiam iniqu't odio habui." *Book of Hours* (Franco-Flemish, fifteenth century). MS. Stowe 17, fol. 106. By permission of the British Library.

5. The Flight into Egypt and the Massacre of the Innocents. *Book of Hours* (Flemish, fifteenth century). MS. Douce 93, fol. 34^{v}. By permission of the Bodleian Library, Oxford.

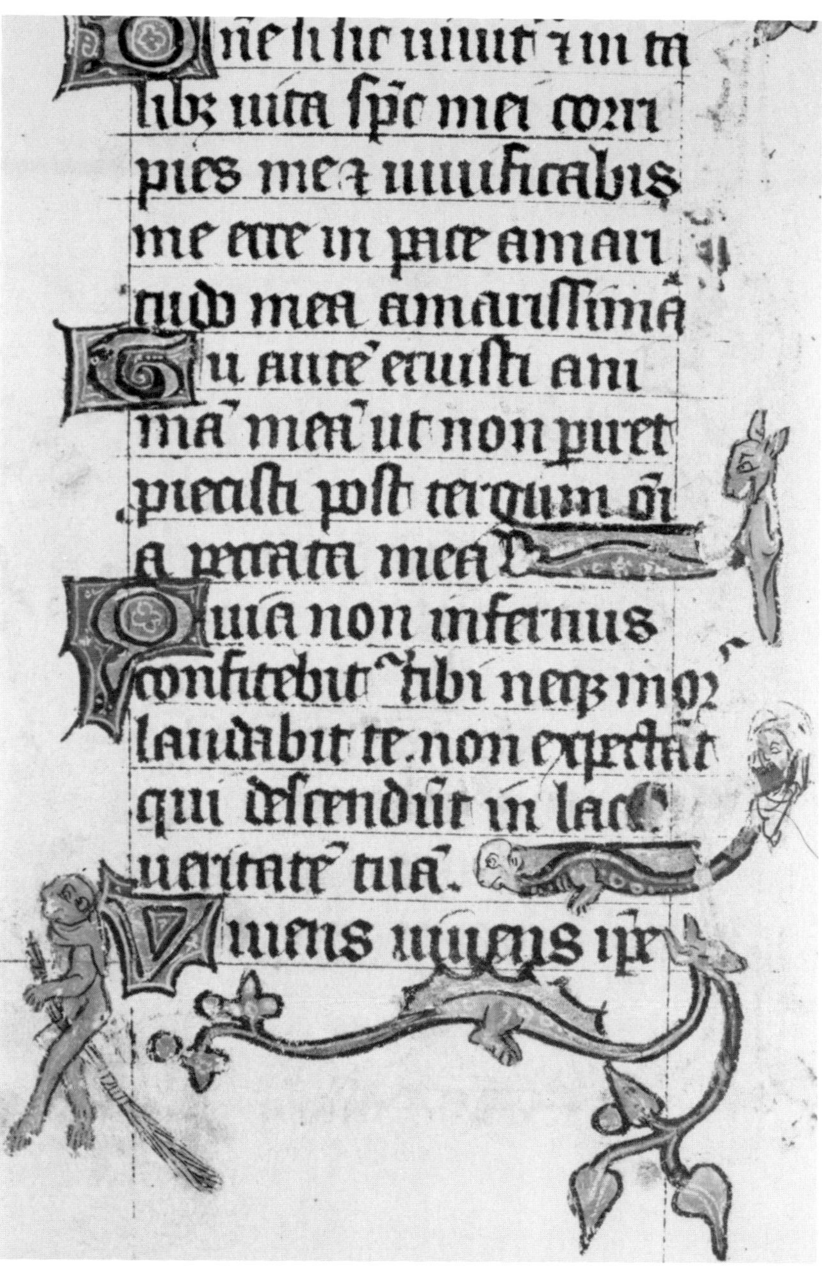

6. Animal marginalia. A donkey wears a clerical red gown and an ape the hood to it. From a *Psalter* (Ghent, 1330–40). MS. GKS 3384, fol. 300^{v}. By permission of the Kongelige Bibliotek, Copenhagen.

7. Fool with tonsure and bauble. Mid-fourteenth century. MS. Douce 211, fol. 258^{v}. By permission of the Bodleian Library, Oxford.

8. An alchemical experiment as an example of folly. Alexander Barclay, *The Ship of Fools* (*STC* 3545), sig. O.iii. By permission of the Folger Shakespeare Library.

9. Juerken, fool of the Antwerp Chamber of Rhetoric De Violieren. Het Landjuweel van 1561. Bibliothèque Royale Albert Ier, MS. II 13.3681 (MS. Van Even), p. 27. By permission of the Bibliothèque Royale, Brussels.

10. Fool, with bauble and bellows, seated on a stool on horseback. Royal Entry of Joanna of Castille, Brussels, 1496. Berlin, Kupferstichkabinett, MS. 75 D 5, fol. 14r. By permission of the Kupferstichkabinett, Staatliche Museen zu Berlin–Preussischer Kulturbesitz.

11. Shrine of Vrou Lorts; fool with bauble in top left hand corner. *Van Nyeuvont, Loosheit ende Practike*, ed. E. Neurdenburg (Utrecht: A. Oosthoek, 1910), fol. B4^{v}.

12. *Temperantia*, with fool holding bauble on stage in upper left. Etching by Ph. Galle after Pieter Bruegel the Elder. Amsterdam, Rijksprentenkabinet B. 138. By permission of the Rijksmuseum, Amsterdam.